FOUNDATIONS OF ISRAEL
Emergence of a Welfare State

OSCAR I. JANOWSKY

Professor of History
The City College of New York

AN ANVIL ORIGINAL
under the general editorship of
LOUIS L. SNYDER

D. VAN NOSTRAND COMPANY, INC.
PRINCETON, NEW JERSEY
TORONTO LONDON
NEW YORK

To

My Children

_____

D. VAN NOSTRAND COMPANY, INC.

120 Alexander St., Princeton, New Jersey (*Principal office*)
257 Fourth Avenue, New York 10, New York
25 Hollinger Rd., Toronto 16, Canada
358, Kensington High Street, London, W.14, England

Library of Congress Catalog Card No. 59-9761

PREFACE

ON Sabbath Eve, the fifth day of the month of Iyar, in the year 5708—May 14, 1948—Israel proclaimed its independence as a sovereign state. (*See Reading No. 22.*) The moment reflected the mood, for Sabbath Eve ever had a stirring effect in Jewish communities. Weekday cares were shed with the well-worn garments, and the hallowed day of rest, the "Sabbath Queen," was ushered in with hymns of praise. The elevation of spirit which Sabbath Eve brought could not but be quickened by the simultaneous appearance of the "Jewish" state after an eclipse of nearly two millennia. Israel's cities and villages resounded with the heavy cadence of the Hora, and the age-old words and chants of the synagogue brightened with new meaning.

The moment evoked another mood. As the sun sank in the western sea, the dangers that lurked on the uncharted borders, and within the borders too, loomed ever larger with the lengthening shadows. Even the historian may permit himself the assumption that harrowing memories of other times and other places pressed into consciousness—the eve of a pogrom in Russia; a night of terror in Nazi Germany. In the new Israel, however, the overpowering emotion was courage, not fear. Anxiety, yes; but not the terror of helplessness and hopelessness. The people and their leaders were determined to hold what they regarded as theirs. Since war was to decide their fate, they were ready to fight.

. . .

The proclamation of the State of Israel, like all momentous events, was at once the culmination of preceding developments and the beginning of a new era. The history of the new state, and the foundations upon which it was reared, are the theme of this volume. But history must ever reckon with antecedents; no event is sufficient unto itself. The institutions of Israel, its aims and ideals, its leadership, even the state of mind of its people are in many respects the products of preceding years. Pertinent historical developments prior to the establishment of Israel will therefore be reviewed.

The aims of this book are to trace the origins and development of Israel and to clarify the purposes which have motivated its architects and protagonists. How it came into being may be grasped with relative ease by following the sequence of known historical events. It is far more difficult and more important to comprehend the spirit of high endeavor which has animated the Israeli Jews, their sense of urgency, their zeal for national regeneration and for the rehabilitation of their ancient homeland. It is likewise necessary, especially in a brief volume, to identify and concentrate attention upon the distinctive features of Israel's development.

These considerations have guided the selection of materials and determined the point of view of the volume. All historical writing inevitably involves selection, which is either purposeful, reflecting an opinion, or the result of the accidents of reading and observation. Here the emphasis is deliberate. The story is unfolded as the development of events, ideas, and institutions: therefore, except for a few leading personalities, names have been omitted. The book is a history of Israel and not of the Middle East nor even of Palestine. It is concerned with the Jews who have built Israel, and the Arabs are considered only in so far as they have affected the course of events which have led to the rise of Israel. Moreover, the central point of reference is the Yishuv (the Jewish community which has evolved in Palestine) with its ideals, strivings, and achievements. And the reader will note an especial concern with the efforts of the Yishuv to foster social idealism and human welfare. Finally, the author regards the theme of this book as a great adventure. He is intrigued by it and considers as highly significant many of the aims and achievements of the Yishuv and of Israel.

I am indebted to numerous authors for insights gained from their books and to several persons for suggestions and for documentary material which would otherwise not have been easily available. I profited from the valuable comments made by Dr. Oskar K. Rabinowicz on Chapters 6-12, and by the Honorable Chaim Cohen of Israel on the material included in Chapters 7-8. Dr. Eliezer Yapou, Counsellor of the Israeli Mission to the United Nations, and Mr. Benjamin Cohen of the Israeli Consulate cheerfully made available documents requested by the author. And the efficient staff of the Zionist Archives and Library of New York eased the task of research. These acknowledgments, however, involve no delegation of responsibility.

OSCAR I. JANOWSKY

TABLE OF CONTENTS

Part I

FOUNDATIONS OF ISRAEL

New York Herald Tribune map—Kavanagh

— 1 —

ORIGINS: JEWS AND PALESTINE BEFORE WORLD WAR I

Origins are points of reference, arbitrarily chosen to clarify later events. The identification of the roots of Israel's problems and policies, or their earlier stages of development, should bring into better focus and illumine present issues and agencies.

The Jews and Palestine. The Jews or Hebrews have been identified with Palestine—the Land of Israel—in fact or by tradition since their patriarchal beginnings. In the Biblical narratives, the ancient Hebrews associated with Palestine (the Land of Canaan) their earliest ancestors who lived centuries before the Hebrews were welded into a people. After the conquest of the country by Moses and Joshua, David (c. 1000 B.C.) consolidated Hebrew power in the land, and for more than a millennium thereafter the Hebrews or Jews inhabited all or parts of what has been called Palestine.

For some 500 or 600 years, the entire Hebrew people dwelt in the Land of Israel (Palestine). In 721 B.C., Israel, the northern kingdom, fell to Assyria, and in 586 B.C., the Babylonians took Judea with its capital, Jerusalem, destroying the Temple built by Solomon. With the exile, first of the northern and then of the southern Hebrews, the Diaspora (dispersion) began, and thereafter an increasing number of Hebrews or Jews lived in Babylonia, Egypt, and elsewhere.

Many of the exiles returned, the Temple was rebuilt in Jerusalem toward the end of the sixth century B.C., and the Second Jewish Commonwealth continued to prosper or to struggle for existence in the midst of contending

empires, until the Romans sacked Jerusalem and burned
the second Temple in 70 A.D. However, even after the
latter date, and down into the fifth century A.D., the
Jews of Palestine enjoyed autonomy, particularly in their
religious and cultural life, but in large measure also in
what would today be regarded as political and social
affairs.

During the Second Jewish Commonwealth, the Diaspora multiplied more rapidly than the Jews of the homeland, so that an ever-growing majority lived outside of
Palestine. Yet the Land of Israel remained the center of
Jewish life, at least until the third century A.D. The large
Jewish communities of the Middle East and the growing
settlements of Asia Minor, Greece, the Balkans, and the
western European lands supported Palestinian institutions
and looked for spiritual guidance to the religious leaders
of the Land of Israel. Moreover, throughout this long
period, Jews in varying numbers continued to return to
what they regarded as their homeland.

The lure of Palestine for the Jews is quite understandable. It was the cradle of their early peoplehood. There
they were welded into what we call today a nation.
National triumphs and catastrophes, perpetuated in
religious lore, remained associated with the hills and
valleys of the little country. Above all, the religious and
literary genius of the Jews blossomed in the Land of
Israel.

It was in Palestine that Hebrews or Jews saw the vision of universal ethical monotheism which reached a
climax in the lofty ideals of peace, justice, and human
brotherhood envisioned by the prophets. The Hebrew
Bible was composed, collected, and canonized in Palestine, and the Bible has endured as the ethical foundation
of the Western and of part of the Eastern World. The
Bible, too, as a collection of literary masterpieces, idealized in poetic imagery the Land of Israel. Other religious
writings, not included in the Bible, were likewise written
in Palestine. It was the seat of the sages who interpreted
the Bible to meet changing conditions, and whose religious and ethical concepts endure in the Mishna and the
Palestinian Talmud.

By the fifth century, A.D., only a small fragment of the
Jews lived in Palestine, and religious and cultural leader-

ship had passed to the Jews of other lands. But the idea persisted that the Jews and the Land of Israel were indissolubly linked. Throughout the Middle Ages, and in modern times as well, small groups of Jews, fired by the ideal of "Return to Zion," migrated from various lands to Palestine in order to live in the Holy Land or at least to be buried in hallowed ground. There is a tradition that at no time during the long centuries was Palestine wholly without a Jewish settlement. At all events, the vast majority of the Jews who remained dispersed in the lands of their adoption—who could not or would not return to Palestine—continued to regard it as their spiritual haven. In prayer and poetic yearning, in synagogue art and in group imagery, the Land of Israel symbolized at once the glory of bygone days and the hope of redemption as a people. It was the link that tied the distant past with the elusive future, with "the end of days," when the Jews and the Land of Israel would again belong to one another. The Land became a symbol of unity for a dispersed people, a rallying point for future nationhood.

The "Return to Zion" Movement. Thus was the stage set for the Return to Zion of the late nineteenth and early twentieth centuries. The impulse came from within the Jewish group, but novel ideas and external pressures altered both the character and objectives of the migration. National striving superseded religious yearning as the compulsive urge, and the ideal of Return to Zion became the lodestone of a modern nationalist movement.

Eastern Europe, notably Russia and Galicia, was the center of the new ferment. National consciousness began to permeate the subject peoples of the Russian and Austro-Hungarian empires during the nineteenth century, the intellectuals taking the lead by probing national origins, idealizing so-called national characteristics, and demanding national unity and independence. This nascent nationalism among young and non-literary peoples had a dual effect in Jewish circles. It turned the minds of literary men to the history and achievements of the Jews as a nation, and they began to see the past in the light of current national concepts. At the same time, the national strivings of the weak and subject peoples among whom they dwelt accentuated the Jews' sense of isolation. In eastern Europe, difference in religion had been and remained a fundamental segregating factor, and to it was now added the divisive force of nationalism. The nationalist spokesmen of the subject peoples, particularly of Czarist Russia, looked either to Pan-Slavism as the unifying principle, or to the ethnic individuality of the particular group. In either case the Jews remained outside the circle of national kinship. Thus the Jews of eastern Europe were an integral part neither of the dominant peoples nor of the various subgroups striving for national recognition. At best they could look forward to a future of acceptance on sufferance.

These inner strivings and environmental influences produced among the Jews of eastern Europe a cultural movement which fostered national consciousness and singled out the Land of Israel as a national haven. And this new orientation transformed the old religious and messianic hope for a Return to Zion into a nationalist ideal to restore the Jews to their old homeland.

External pressures quickened these nationalist stirrings among the Jews into an organized movement to return to Palestine. In 1881 a series of organized massacres (pogroms) in south Russia shocked the civilized world and convinced many Jews that Czarist Russia held no future for them. A strong current of emigrants turned to America, but national consciousness deflected a not inconsiderable number to Palestine. This wave of immigration (known as the First *Aliya*) continued from 1882 to 1903 and brought some 25,000 Jews to Palestine. The large majority were Russian Jews, with a contingent from Rumania, where conditions were no more promising than in Russia. The new immigrants found in Palestine an old settlement of some 24,000 Jews, dedicated to pious observance and subsisting in the main in utter poverty from charitable collections secured in Europe and elsewhere. The newcomers began to transform the character of the Jewish population of Palestine. By 1903, however, the Zionist movement had been launched by Theodor Herzl, who was galvanized into action by external pressures.

Theodor Herzl and Organized Zionism. Herzl was a successful Viennese journalist and man of letters thoroughly at home in "Western" society. He was unaffected by the Jewish nationalist ferment outlined above and un-

concerned about Palestine. He was troubled by the linger-
ing prejudice against the Jews even after legal equality
had been proclaimed, and he hoped that assimilation
would put an end to "the invisible ghetto." However, the
new anti-Semitism, blatant in Germany and especially
rampant in Vienna, shocked him, because it repudiated
the Jews as racially inferior and called for their segrega-
tion and isolation. The crisis in his thinking occurred in
Paris, whither he had come as representative of a liberal
Viennese newspaper and where he witnessed the bitter
hatred engendered by the Dreyfus Affair. A sensitive
man, he was shaken deeply by the spectacle of Jew-baiting
in Paris, the home of Jewish emancipation. Undergoing
an emotional and intellectual crisis, he emerged with a
plan (embodied in a book, entitled *Der Judenstaat*) for
the restoration of a Jewish state.

For the implementation of his plan, Herzl first sought
the aid of men of wealth and influence; but he was
quickly disillusioned and turned to the Jewish masses,
who rallied to his support especially in eastern Europe.
He called a Zionist Congress which met in Basle, Switzerland, in August, 1897. The Congress resolved to create
for the Jewish people a home in Palestine. This came to
be known as the "Basle Program." (*See Reading No. 1.*)

With the Basle Congress, the Zionist Organization came
into being. The Congress, meeting periodically, was the
supreme authority in the Zionist movement. Herzl was
elected president, and executive bodies were empowered
to direct affairs in the intervals between meetings of the
Congress. An official organ, *Die Welt*, and other publications expounded the Zionist idea, Zionist societies sprang
up in various countries, and financial institutions were
soon established for the practical work of the movement.

Herzl was a dynamic leader and worked indefatigably.
But his efforts to secure a charter from the Turkish
sultan and to enlist the aid of the powers proved fruitless,
and he burned himself out in a few years, dying in 1904
at the age of 44. But the movement he launched endured.

Herzl's activities and the development of the Zionist
movement set in motion a new wave of immigration from
Russia (the Second *Aliya*) which brought to Palestine
some 40,000 Jews between 1904 and 1914. This element,

politically and nationally self-conscious, had the most
profound influence on the future of Jewish Palestine, as
will be indicated in due course.

— 2 —

THE BALFOUR DECLARATION AND THE PALESTINE MANDATE

World War I proved decisive in the history of Zionism,
bringing in its train first a major crisis and then apparent
victory. Suspicious and hostile, the Turkish authorities
threatened to destroy what the Jews had wrought in
Palestine. Deportations and disease reduced the Jewish
population of about 85,000 at the outbreak of the war to
some 56,000 in 1918. However, the British Government
issued the Balfour Declaration (November 2, 1917),
pledging to facilitate "the establishment in Palestine of a
national home for the Jewish People." (*See Reading No.
2.*) And by the end of the war, the British had conquered
the country and were in position to fulfill the pledge.

The Paris Peace Conference of 1919 decided that
Palestine should become a Mandate, to be administered
by a trustee or mandatory government, and in the following year, Britain was designated the mandatory. The
terms of the Mandate were confirmed by the Council of
the League of Nations in 1922 and declared in effect on
September 29, 1923. The Mandate recognized "the
historical connection of the Jewish people with Palestine"
and "the grounds for reconstituting their national home
in that country." Britain was to encourage the immigration and close settlement of Jews on the land; Hebrew, as
well as English and Arabic, was to be an official language;
and a "Jewish Agency" was to be established to "assist and
take part in the development of the country" and to ad-

vise and cooperate with the British authorities in the building of the Jewish National Home. (*See Reading No. 3.*) The Jewish National Home, envisaged by the Balfour Declaration, thus attained international sanction through the agency of the League of Nations. However, the provisions relating to the Jewish National Home were limited to western Palestine, the territory east of the Jordan (Transjordan) having been specifically excluded by the British Government.

The United States stood aloof from the League of Nations and its Mandates, but it, too, signified approval. The Joint Congressional Resolution of June 30, 1922, adopted unanimously by both houses of Congress, declared in favor of the Jewish National Home. (*See Reading No. 4.*) Similarly, the American-British Convention of December, 1924, included and indicated acceptance of the provisions of the Palestine Mandate, secured equal rights for American citizens, and stipulated the requirement of American assent to any changes which might affect the rights of Americans.

These political triumphs of Zionism were indeed extraordinary but not sufficient for the building of the Jewish National Home. The task was prodigious, requiring large-scale Jewish immigration and extensive economic development for its absorption. But such far-reaching efforts required governmental powers, and these were unattainable so long as the Jewish population of Palestine remained a relatively small minority. This circle of frustration plagued the architects of the Jewish National Home throughout the period of the Mandate. The primary obstacles were the land, the British administration, and especially the indigenous population.

Palestine Undeveloped. The land of Palestine was small and by modern standards quite barren, with the limited stretches of fertile soil depleted by human neglect. Forests had disappeared, top soil had been washed away, and stagnant waters had converted productive valleys into festering marshes. For centuries the desert and the sea had been allowed to encroach upon the habitable land, piling sand dunes upon the coast and nibbling away morsels of precious soil.

Industry was practically non-existent. Mineral resources remained unexploited and unexplored. Standards of production and of living were primitive. This stagnant economy militated against the building of the Jewish National Home. Immigration was the keystone of that undertaking, but without economic development the country could barely sustain its native population. We must repeat that governmental powers were necessary for planned and comprehensive economic expansion. But it was the British and not the Jews who wielded the powers of government. The burden of developing absorptive capacity for immigration was left to the Jews.

British Policy. Years of controversy embittered relations between Britain and the proponents of the Jewish National Home, especially Palestine Jewry. The Balfour Declaration and the terms of the Mandate engendered hopes of a rapid realization of the National Home, and hope quickened zeal. But the British administration served as a brake on Jewish efforts. Charges were therefore heard that Britain was hostile to the Jewish National Home. Individual Britishers, both at home and in Palestine, were, indeed, hostile to Zionism, but official policy was not. The charges of ill will issued from the mistaken assumption that Britain was in Palestine to further the Jewish National Home.

Britain's primary aim in Palestine was to advance imperial interests, notably to safeguard imperial and Commonwealth communications and to assure the uninterrupted flow of oil which was assuming ever greater significance in its economy and defense. Jewish national aspirations were secondary, if that.

Imperial interests required peace and stability in the Middle East, with tractable and loyal if not wholly contented native populations and governments. If the Jewish National Home could be built without disturbing the tranquillity of Palestine and the Middle East, British good will would, no doubt, have been a constant encouragement. Once Arab opposition flared up in riots and bloodshed which had to be suppressed, imperial interests were threatened through the alienation of the natives in Palestine and neighboring countries. The British authorities, therefore, sought to placate the Arabs by restraining Jewish efforts. And instead of encouraging immigration and close settlement of Jews upon the land, in accord with the terms of the Mandate, Britain assumed a position of neutrality, vacillating between opposing pressures of Jews and Arabs and balancing the demands of each against the other.

The commitments of the Balfour Declaration and the Mandate lent themselves to a policy of balance. The former declared in favor of a Jewish National Home, but it also stipulated that "nothing shall be done which may prejudice the civil and religious rights of existing non-Jewish communities in Palestine. . . ." The Mandate, too, while obligating the British to facilitate Jewish immigration and close settlement on the land, required the Palestine administration to ensure "that the rights and position of other sections of the population are not prejudiced." Therefore, as the struggle between Arabs and Jews sharpened, the emphasis of British policy shifted away from the requirements of the Jewish National Home and toward the protection of Arab rights. The negative stipulation which had first appeared as a limiting safeguard in the building of a Jewish National Home came to outweigh in British policy the positive injunction to further its achievement.

However, until 1939, Britain did not repudiate the commitment for a Jewish National Home, despite Arab insurrection, and the foundations of the National Home were laid while the British were masters of the land. Only in 1939, when world war loomed menacingly, and after Czechoslovakia had been sacrificed on the altar of appeasement, did Britain determine to abandon its pledge. The Jewish National Home was never more than a secondary consideration of British policy in Palestine, and when imperial interests appeared to require its abandonment, the British did not hesitate. But for two decades, the decision was not taken, and the Jews were enabled to consolidate a position of considerable strength.

The Arab Population. The Arabs presented the most formidable obstacle to Jewish aspirations. To the newcomer, the country appeared empty, with its barren hills, marshy valleys, a coastline dotted with sand dunes, and a vast and virtually uninhabited southland. However, Palestine was far from empty. In 1922, about 668,000 non-Jews lived in its towns and villages, among them over 100,000 nomad Bedouins whose mode of life had not changed since the time of Mohammed. The Arabs had conquered Palestine in the seventh century A.D., and though subject to alien rule for long periods, uninterrupted possession of the soil for thirteen centuries provided deep rootage and a feeling of permanence.

Jewish nationalist aspirations were irritating to the Arabs because they portended radical changes in the old ways, and especially because they clashed with tradition which had relegated Jews to an inferior status in all Arab lands. And tradition in the Middle East was sanctified by religion as the will of God. The relatively few Oriental Jews who lived in Palestine and knew their place as inferiors did not affect the existing order of things. Even the "old settlement" of European Jewish pietists who had arrived or continued to come in insignificant numbers might be tolerated, for their concern was with ancient lore and ritual observance which did not disturb accepted norms and statuses. But the new immigrants who came to build a Jewish National Home defied tradition. They established themselves "as of right and not on sufferance," and their economic status, education, manner of living, and behavior belied the assumption of Moslem superiority. The cultural clash was deep and disturbing.

Arab Nationalism. These barely conscious irritations of the masses were given expression and direction by the Arab elite who became imbued with a nationalism of their own after World War I. A discussion of Arab nationalism would take us far afield; here it is sufficient to indicate that its basic objective was to rid the country of foreign domination. The nationalist leaders still thought in terms of family rather than national loyalties, and bitter feuds were not uncommon. But to all Arab nationalists, the Balfour Declaration was anathema, the Mandate an imposition, and Jewish immigration an intrusion. In the ideal of the Jewish National Home they saw no more than an effort to wrest the country from its owners.

All arguments, all Jewish efforts to reassure them were fruitless. It is true that early in 1919, at the time of the Paris Peace Conference, an understanding was reached with the Amir Faisal, spokesman of the Arabs. In negotiations with Chaim Weizmann, leader of the Zionists, he agreed to support all measures which would "afford the fullest guarantees for carrying into effect" the Balfour Declaration, including large scale Jewish immigration into

Palestine. But this was contingent upon the realization of Arab aims for a greater Arab state. When the latter failed, the agreement lapsed. At all events, the entire episode was soon forgotten.

The Jews paid fabulously high prices for the land which they acquired, and leading Arab families were not averse to selling land to them. Provision was made for Arab cultivators who were displaced by Jewish purchases of land. The Arabs benefited from Jewish medical and sanitary installations. Arab wages and earnings were far higher in Palestine than in neighboring Arab lands, because of Jewish immigration and enterprise.

The Jews argued that economic development would increase manifold the absorptive capacity of the country; that it would create greater opportunities and sources of a better life and livelihood for Arabs as well as for Jewish immigrants. All to no effect. The Arab nationalists wanted no Jewish National Home, even if that meant curtailed opportunities for Arabs. They clamored for estoppage of Jewish immigration. At best they would tolerate only a small Jewish minority, subject to their rule. Relying on superior numbers, they resorted to violence and threatened to drive the Jews into the sea.

The more immediate Arab-Jewish conflict created the impression that Arab disaffection was not directed against British rule. In fact, however, this was not so. Arab nationalism in Palestine was part of Middle Eastern resentment against alien domination. The French in Syria had to cope with insurrection in the 1920's. The British were compelled to make concessions in Iraq until the latter won qualified independence and admission to the League of Nations in 1932. Ibn Saud of Arabia defied the British and drove their puppet from Mecca. Egypt was in continuous ferment after World War I, wringing concessions from the British until it too achieved "independence" and membership in the League of Nations in 1937. All this emboldened the Palestine Arabs to challenge the British authorities. But the occasion and the rallying cry was the Jewish National Home.

Arab Violence and British Concessions. The Arab leaders were in a position to make good their threat of violence. Emotions flare quickly in the Middle East, and religious sensibilities are especially touchy. It was there-

fore a simple matter for the nationalist leaders to inflame
the city mobs against the Jews.

Even before the Mandate was confirmed by the League
of Nations, rioting broke out, first in Jerusalem in April,
1920, and then, in May, 1921, in more bloody form in
Jaffa. To reassure the Arabs and to serve imperial interests, the British isued the Churchill White Paper of 1922,
a clarifying statement which curtailed Jewish hopes. The
statement of policy explained that the Jews were in
Palestine "as of right and not on sufferance." But the
aim of the National Home was "not the imposition of a
Jewish nationality upon the inhabitants of Palestine as a
whole, but the further development of the existing Jewish
community, with the assistance of Jews in other parts of
the world, in order that it may become a centre in which
the Jewish people as a whole may take, on grounds of
religion and race, an interest and a pride." Jewish immigration was to continue, with the proviso that the
volume be governed by the economic absorptive capacity
of the country.

To the British, this appeared a fair compromise, a
middle course between the contending claims. But it only
alarmed the Jews and failed to placate the Arabs, who
were impervious to any compromise. For a time relative
quiet prevailed, partly because economic crisis reduced
Jewish immigration and partly out of respect for a
vigorous High Commissioner who held office from 1925
to 1928. In the following year, however, a burst of
violence, fanned by religious zeal, took the lives of 133
Jews, including women and children. The newcomers,
who knew how to defend themselves, held their own. It
was the "old settlement" of defenseless pietists, mainly in
Hebron and Safed, who were done to death in savage
attacks.

The reaction of the British Government was one of
impatience with the troublesome problems of the Jewish
National Home. A Commission of Inquiry was dispatched, and it found that the Jewish National Home occasioned resentment among the Arabs. Moreover, it
tended to emphasize the provisions of the Mandate which
sought to safeguard the rights of the non-Jewish population, and relegated to the background the positive requirements of the Mandate for the encouragement of the

Jewish National Home. The Commission favored more stringent regulation of Jewish immigration and land purchases and called for a new statement of policy to define and safeguard Arab rights. Even more ominous for Jewish hopes were the temporary suspension of Jewish labor immigration and the findings of a British expert, who reported after a hasty survey that with prevailing methods of cultivation, there was no margin of land available for the settlement of new immigrants, and that even with extensive economic development, about 20,000 immigrant families might be settled on the land. He also cast doubt on the soundness of Jewish efforts by questioning the value of Jewish industrial development and the social experiments of Jewish labor.

The Mandates Commission of the League of Nations, which considered the Palestine question in June, 1930, warned against the obvious trend in British policy. It censured the Mandatory for its inadequate security measures during the riots of 1929, and questioned the assumption that the latter were not directed against British authority. It also held that the Mandatory had neither given the Jews sufficient aid in building the National Home nor helped the Arabs by adequate agricultural development. Finally, it cautioned the British not to yield to the demands of those who were rebelling against the Mandate.

These warnings were disregarded, and the British Government issued a "definitive" statement of policy in the White Paper of 1930. This constricted sharply the opportunities for building the Jewish National Home. It underscored the "double undertaking" of the Mandate—to the Arabs as well as the Jews—and declared categorically that no more land was available for Jewish agricultural settlement. Immigration was not wholly excluded, but economic absorptive capacity, stringently defined, was to serve as an effective check. And the harsh and petulant tone of this policy statement was especially irritating to the Jews, as it seemingly confirmed their fears that the British were determined to placate the Arabs at the cost of Jewish interests. The Arabs, however, remained unappeased.

Refugee Pressure and British Hesitation. If the British Government had really decided to put a stop to im-

migration, external pressures upon European Jewry
quickly set such plans at nought. Hitler came to power in
1933, and the German Jews began to flee from the Nazi
inferno. No country welcomed the fugitives, some of
whom were hounded like beasts at the guarded frontiers.
Palestine simply could not close its doors to them. Over
104,000 entered the country during 1934-1935. Industry
and agriculture grew rapidly, and tension mounted. The
British Government hoped to mollify the Arabs by
further curtailment of Jewish rights. They talked of restricting land sales to Jews and of scrutinizing absorptive
capacity more closely, and proposed a Legislative Council
with an Arab majority. But opposition in Parliament and
in Palestine induced further hesitation.

The British Government was ready to halt the development of the National Home by indirection but not by
downright repudiation. The situation, however, had so
deteriorated that only a bold policy, one way or the
other, might have maintained the peace. And boldness was
wanting in the British Governments of the 1930's. Military unpreparedness and the challenges of Hitler and
Mussolini produced a policy of concession and accommodation in western Europe, in the Mediterranean and
the Middle East. In the late 1930's, vacillation in Palestine was a phase of British world policy, and it cost them
the respect of the Arabs as well as the confidence of the
Jews.

Arab Revolt and the Peel Commission. In the spring
of 1936, riots broke out in Jaffa and spread rapidly. Yet
another commission of inquiry, the Peel Commission, was
sent to Palestine in the hope of finding a solution.

This commission came to grips with the problem. Reporting in 1937, it found that the Mandate involved
obligations to Jews and Arabs, but denied the premise of
equality of obligations: "Unquestionably," said the Report, "the primary purpose of the Mandate, *as expressed
in its preamble and its articles,* is to promote the establishment of the Jewish National Home." Furthermore, it
recognized in absorptive capacity a dynamic process, with
immigration and the influx of capital actually increasing
the possibilities of further immigration. However, the opposition of the Arabs made the Mandate unworkable. The
aspirations of the Jews and Arabs were irreconcilable in

a united Palestine, but the commission saw justice in both claims and recommended partition—a division of the country into a Jewish State, an Arab State, and a permanent British mandate over specified areas.

The Jews gave the principle of partition qualified support and stood ready to negotiate on the terms of implementation. But the Arabs, emboldened by Fascist and Nazi encouragement, would not hear of partition, and violence flared in open rebellion. The British Government vacillated. At first it approved the principle of partition, but Arab intransigence occasioned reconsideration. Another commission was appointed to elaborate a detailed plan, and its findings proved partition unworkable and unacceptable to all parties. The Government thereupon withdrew its endorsement of partition.

The Scuttling of the Mandate. By this time, Neville Chamberlain was Prime Minister and appeasement was the formula which was to secure "peace for our time." With Czechoslovakia thrown to the Nazis, could the Jewish National Home long endure?

Early in 1939, a "round-table" conference was convoked in London of representatives of the Jews, the Palestine Arabs, and—a novel step—of the neighboring Arab states. The Arabs refused to meet with the Jews, and British negotiations with both parties proved fruitless. The British Government thereupon produced its own plan, announcing it as official policy in the White Paper of May, 1939. (*See Reading No. 5.*) This, said the Chamberlain Government, was "an alternative policy [to take the place of partition] which will, consistently with their obligations to Arabs and Jews, meet the needs of the situation in Palestine."

The new plan was no more than the culmination of the previous tendency to whittle down Jewish rights and halt the building of the National Home by indirection, safeguarding, at the same time, British imperial interests. The provisions were as follows:

(1) After an interval of ten years, an independent Palestine state (predominantly Arab) would be set up, with proper assurances for the commercial and strategic requirements of Great Britain. The British Government, however, reserved the right to postpone indefinitely the establishment of this state.

(2) A constitution was to be elaborated by a conference to be convoked five years after the restoration of order. And the constitution was to incorporate safeguards for the Holy Places, the Jewish National Home, and British imperial interests.

(3) Jewish immigration, unless approved by the Palestine Arabs, was to come to an end after five years. In the interval beginning with April, 1939, immigration was to be limited to 10,000 yearly, and this, too, was to be subject to absorptive capacity. An additional 25,000 *refugees* might be admitted, if the High Commissioner was assured of their proper maintenance. In other words, a total of 75,000 Jews were to be admitted between 1939-1944, and thereafter the Jewish National Home was to be shut tight even to Jewish refugees, unless the Arabs approved.

(4) The High Commissioner would be empowered "to prohibit and regulate" the transfer or sale of land by Arabs to Jews.

A certain naive ingenuity characterized the policy of the White Paper. The Jewish National Home was not openly repudiated. Indeed, the pretense was maintained that it was being preserved: lip service was paid to it in the White Paper, and it was to be "safeguarded" in the projected constitution of the contemplated Palestine State. However, immigration and land purchase, with close settlement on the land, were the twin pillars of the National Home, and both were knocked down by the Chamberlain Government, leaving a partially reared superstructure which could not endure.

Recognizing the centrality of immigration and settlement on the land, the authors of the Mandate had stipulated that "the Administration of Palestine, while ensuring that the rights and position of other sections of the population are not prejudiced, shall facilitate Jewish immigration . . . and shall encourage . . . close settlement by Jews on the land, including State lands and waste lands not required for public purposes." Both were denied to the Jews, and yet the White Paper asserted that its policy was consistent with Britain's obligations to Arabs and Jews. The heavy-handed smugness of the White Paper was especially revealed by the claim—self-deluding, if honestly held—that it would meet "the needs of the situation in Palestine." The White Paper satisfied neither the Jews nor the Arabs nor the Mandates Commission which had the authority to advise the Council of the League of Nations on all matters relating to the observ-ance of the Mandate.

The Permanent Mandates Commission examined the policy of the White Paper in June, 1939, and reported its observations to the League Council. (*See Reading No. 6.*) It found unanimously "that the policy set out in the White Paper was not in accordance with the interpretation which, in agreement with the mandatory Power and the Council, the Commission had always placed upon the Palestine mandate." Furthermore, while three of the seven members then in attendance believed that the new policy could be justified by existing circumstances, "pro-vided the Council did not oppose it," the majority of the Commission declared, in the mild and circumspect lan-guage characteristic of that body, that they were unable "to state that the policy of the White Paper was in con-formity with the mandate, any contrary conclusion ap-pearing to them to be ruled out by the very terms of the mandate and by the fundamental intentions of its au-thors." In plain words, the majority held that the White Paper violated the principles of the Mandate. Indeed it did, for, apart from the clear injunctions relating to the National Home, Article 15 of the Mandate had stipulated that ". . . no discrimination of any kind shall be made between the inhabitants of Palestine on the ground of race, religion or language. No person shall be excluded from Palestine on the sole ground of his religious belief."

Modification of the terms of the Mandate required the consent of the League Council. But the outbreak of World War II resulted in the suspension of League activi-ties. The Council therefore never gave legal sanction to the policy of the White Paper, which remained an arbi-trary act of the mandatory. The British Government, however, ignored the legal question and pressed on with the implementation of its policy.

In February, 1940, the Land Transfers Regulations were issued (*see Reading No. 7*), tightening the restric-tive policy of the White Paper of 1939: what the latter did to Jewish immigration, the former even more effec-tively did to land purchases by Jews. The country was

divided into zones. The transfer of land to Jews was
entirely prohibited in Zone A, which embraced 4,104,000
acres and constituted 63.1% of the total area of Palestine.
In Zone B (2,067,840 acres, 31.8% of the country)
transfers of land might be effected only with the consent
of the High Commissioner, and in fact no such consent
was ever given. The unrestricted Zone comprised the
urban areas, part of the maritime plain, and the Haifa
industrial district. Here the Jews could purchase land
freely, but it should be noted that this zone constituted no
more than 5.1% of the area of Palestine, and that Jews
already owned about one-half of its 332,160 acres. In
effect, the Regulations left open to possible purchase by
Jews approximately 166,000 acres. To be sure, the Land
Transfers Regulations appeared to leave open the pos-
sibility of transfer of public lands to the Jews. A saving
and soothing clause declared that "nothing in these regulations shall be deemed . . . to apply to the transfer of
any public lands by or on behalf of the High Commissioner." The disingenuousness of this promise was soon
revealed when the latter ruled that "ordinarily" the
restrictions would apply to public lands, too. And, in fact
no Jews, not even veterans who served with the British
during World War II, ever received a grant or lease of
public land.

    Reaction of Jews and Arabs. The Jews were aghast.
They saw their promised National Home reduced to a
mockery, for the National Home was to be one of the
few countries left in the world into which Jews as Jews
could not immigrate; one of the few areas in which land
purchase was denied them. They were asked to forget the
lofty vision of a National Home evoked by the Balfour
Declaration and the Mandate, and to accept as the reality
a ghetto with medieval adornments.

    The scuttling of the National Home, the hypocritical lan-
guage, and the patent illegality of the White Paper and
land regulations embittered the Jews. Another factor, the
urge to self-preservation, lashed them to fury. It must be
remembered that all this happened in 1939 and 1940,
after the Nazis had seized Austria and Czechoslovakia
and overun western Poland. Literally millions of Jews
were in the grip of unparalleled terror, with flight the
only alternative to slaughter. Fugitives streamed to all

borders, but few avenues of escape remained open, and no country offered permanent haven.

It should be noted, too, that for Palestine's Jews, the victims of the Nazis were not distant and vague creatures whose fate might be deplored or dismissed with a sigh or an oath. They were flesh and blood to them—parents, brothers, sisters, friends—and many Palestine Jews had intimate knowledge of the horrors suffered at the hands of the Nazis. That the Jewish National Home should be shut tight against the remnant that might be saved appeared to the Jews a crime against a law higher than that of the Chamberlain government. And this was not the mood of extremists but the expression of a people's despair.

The pent up frustration and resentment of the Jews erupted in open defiance. They refused to recognize the "illegal" policy of the White Paper and organized immigration in the teeth of government regulations. The government retaliated by suspending legal immigration (from October, 1939, to March, 1940, and from October, 1940, to March, 1941), and the issue was squarely joined.

If the new regulations had satisfied the Arabs, Englishmen might perhaps have found justification in the thought that imperial interests were better served. But the Arabs were no more appeased by the anti-Jewish policy than was Hitler by the rape of Czechoslovakia. The obvious abandonment of the Jewish National Home was indeed welcome to them, but that was not the limit of their demands; only the British nourished that illusion. The Arabs wanted to be rid of the British as well as the Jews. In the promised Palestine state, which the British government reserved the right to postpone indefinitely, they recognized a shallow imperialist disguise, and imperialism in any form had become anathema. Their intransigence had yielded results. Why not continue the pressure? They therefore remained sullen and defiant, and in the midst of world war, the British were obliged to use military force to maintain their precarious position. The bankruptcy of the Chamberlain policy was as complete in Palestine as in Europe.

— 3 —

PALESTINE AND WORLD WAR II

Plight of Refugees. World War II taxed the states-
manship of Palestine Jewish leadership. The White Paper
policy was brutally enforced. On the eve of the war, the
Jews petitioned that 30,000 children and youth from the
areas threatened by Hitler be admitted as part of the
75,000 which the White Paper had conceded. The petition was denied. We have already seen that in 1939 and
again in 1940 the Palestine administration suspended for
periods of six months the trifling legal immigration, in
punishment of the illegal entry of Jews. When refugees
continued to arrive, despite warnings and threats, the
British government inaugurated, toward the end of 1940,
the policy of hustling them off and interning them elsewhere, with the stern warning that they would never be
admitted to Palestine. In the midst of total war, British
naval craft took time out to patrol the Palestine coast
and intercept miserable refugees crowded on decrepit
vessels.

The determined policy of the British occasioned a
number of terrible and dramatic tragedies. The ship
Patria was intercepted in November, 1940, with 1771
unauthorized immigrants to Palestine, and the refugees
were held on board in Haifa harbor for deportation. The
ship blew up and over 200 Jews were lost. Fugitives from
the Nazi inferno were reaching Istanbul, and the Jews
begged that they be given refuge in the Jewish National
Home. The British not only refused but also pressed the
Turkish government to deny them passage through its
land and territorial waters. The homeless and terrified
beings pressed on, however, with the encouragement of
Palestine Jewry and of other Jews as well. If they could
enter legally, proper means of transportation would have
been provided. Illegal sailing placed valuable ships out
of reach, and any vessel, no matter how unseaworthy,

held the hope of escape for the hapless victims. Panic resulted in overcrowding, because the fugitives feared the long reach of Nazi malevolence. Some miraculously reached Palestine, eluding the net spread by the British authorities. Others paid with their lives for their desperate courage. The *Salvador,* an unseaworthy vessel, went down in the seas south of Istanbul, and over 200, many of them children, perished. The *Struma,* small and unseaworthy, reached Istanbul with 769 fugitives, far more than the vessel could hold. It was detained by the Turkish government in accord with their commitment to the British, while the Jews pleaded that the refugees be admitted to Palestine under the legal quota of the White Paper. The British were adamant, and after two months the ship, lacking food and provisions, was ordered on February 23, 1942 to return to the Black Sea. It sank on the same day, carrying to their death all but one of the passengers.

Jewish Support of War Effort. These harrowing events and the callousness of the British authorities enraged the Jews, and one might have expected a Jewish rising in Palestine. A small group did resort to terrorism, but among the population as a whole national discipline held. The leaders counseled individual restraint and elaborated a threefold policy, namely: (1) illegal immigration was encouraged in defiance of the British authorities; (2) the cooperation of Palestine Jewry in fighting the war was offered the British Government; and (3) the desires of the Jews for a National Home hardened into a demand for statehood.

The Jews of Palestine had no choice in the matter of the war. Regardless of Britain's hostile policy, Hitler was still the supreme enemy. They therefore declared their solidarity with the Allied cause and pressed the Government to form a Jewish army for service wherever needed; over 130,000 Jewish men and women registered for war service. In 1941, the Churchill cabinet approved this proposal in principle, but the opposition of the British authorities in Egypt and Palestine prevented its realization until 1944, when a Jewish Brigade was at last organized. Even before that, some 24,000 Palestine Jews had enlisted in the British forces and in time served in the Middle East and in Europe.

The Jewish civilian population of Palestine, with its industrial equipment, its technicians, its scientists and medical men, made it possible to utilize the country as a war arsenal. Land mines and tank engines, small naval craft and precision instruments, clothing and medical supplies were produced in Palestine, and it became a repair depot for heavier equipment. The Hebrew University provided sera for the treatment of typhus and other diseases. Its meteorological department supplied weather data covering the entire Middle East. And at the request of the British, the Hebrew University and Hadassah arranged courses in tropical medicine and war surgery for several hundred medical officers of the British forces. The Technical Institute of Haifa and the Research Institute at Rehovot likewise rendered specialized scientific services to the British war effort.

The Biltmore Program. At the same time, the Jews sharpened their demands for a postwar settlement. The concept of the Jewish National Home had held the promise of peaceful growth and of some form of political cooperation between Jews and Arabs. But the Arabs had repudiated it in any and every form, and the White Paper of 1939 had emptied it of significant content. The National Home had become a delusion and a taunt, and the Jews were determined that the survivors of Nazi savagery should find haven in Palestine. The fate of the refugees who were allowed to perish even after eluding the tentacles of the Nazis tore to shreds the last vestiges of confidence in Britain. The demand for a Jewish state gained in volume and intensity, and while formulated by the Zionist executive in Palestine, it first achieved public expression in the United States.

In May, 1942, an Extraordinary Zionist Conference was held at the Hotel Biltmore in New York, with Weizmann, Ben Gurion, and other leading Zionists in attendance. This conference urged "that the gates of Palestine be opened; that the Jewish Agency be vested with control of immigration into Palestine and with the necessary authority for upbuilding the country, . . . and that Palestine be established as a Jewish Commonwealth integrated in the structure of the new democratic world." This came to be known as the Biltmore Program, which was officially adopted by the American Zionist Organization and by the General Council of the World Zionist Organization in the fall of 1942, and confirmed by the Representative Assembly of Palestine Jewry two years later.

The Arabs and the War. The White Paper policy of the British Government was callous and harsh, but it was not the expression of hatred of Jews, even of Palestine Jewry. Impatience and annoyance, yes; but not hatred. It was aimed to secure the loyalty of the Arabs in the war, and in this, it proved an illusion.

British military power kept the Palestine Arabs quiet, but they remained sullen and uncooperative. The neighboring Arab states, however, were openly hostile. In Egypt, the king made manifest his anti-British feelings; the minister of defense turned over military secrets to Britain's Italian enemy; and in 1942, the British were obliged to dictate a change in the Egyptian government. Syria was rife with pro-Nazi feeling. And in Iraq a serious pro-Nazi rising, suppressed by the British, elicited widespread support in the Arab world. It was only in 1945, when Nazi defeat appeared certain, that Egypt, Saudi Arabia, Syria, and Lebanon declared war against the Germans and were able soon thereafter to become charter members of the United Nations.

Imperialist hopes die hard. The British ignored the war service of Palestine Jewry and overlooked Arab disloyalty. Despite the war experience, they still believed that they could maintain ascendancy in the Middle East with Arab acquiescence. Before the war was over, the British helped forge an instrument of Arab unity which later contributed to their own undoing. In March, 1945, a League of Arab States was formed in Cairo with British encouragement, and this Arab League declared that Palestine was an Arab country which had been assured independence in the White Paper of 1939. The future of British imperial policy, like its past, would apparently base its hopes on Arab support.

*   *   *

By the end of World War II, the conflict over the Jewish National Home had reached deadlock. Arab and Jewish aspirations were clearly irreconcilable; the British had thrown their weight against the Jews; and head-on

collision appeared inevitable. The following years were
to see decisive developments, but before proceeding, it
will be helpful to pause and describe what the Jews had
accomplished in the building of their National Home.

— 4 —

BUILDING THE JEWISH NATIONAL HOME

The opposition of the Arabs and the policies of the
British authorities posed formidable obstacles to the building of the Jewish National Home. The periodic disturbances and the commissions of inquiry which ensued commanded close attention. Much effort had to be expended
in compiling evidence, defending policies, and pleading
the Jewish cause in Palestine, in England, and elsewhere.

However, the best energies of the Jews were devoted
to constructive work, and despite all hindrances, remarkable progress was made. The Jewish population grew and
was absorbed in an expanding economy. Provision was
made for health, education, and welfare. Parts of the
country assumed a Jewish character, with distinctive national-cultural features. And an organized community
emerged as representative of and spokesman for Palestine
Jewry. By the end of World War II, Palestine Jewry—
or the *Yishuv,* as it was generally called—had achieved
sufficient strength to meet the challenge to the National
Home.

We shall trace briefly the development of the basic
components of the Jewish National Home, namely, population and immigration, economic growth, the organized
Jewish community and its social and cultural assets; and
the attempt will be made to identify the distinctive features of the Jewish National Home.

The Problem of Development. The British authorities, who ruled the country from the end of World War I until 1948, introduced honest and efficient administration and some of the essential government services they thought necessary for a "colonial" population. The administrative apparatus, central and local, the security forces, taxation, and the courts were reorganized. A customs service was introduced, but not a comprehensive protective tariff for industrial development. Postal, telephone, and telegraph services were modernized. The railways were improved and some motor roads built.

Agriculture, notably Arab agriculture, was in need of extensive aid. But the British administration provided little more than supervision and guidance; it did not regard it as its function to tamper with the class structure of native society or the time-honored system of land tenure. An agricultural department sought to limit the effects of drought, pests, and plant and cattle diseases. Demonstration farms and forest nurseries were established for agricultural guidance. A cadastral survey was made and laws enacted to protect the tenant cultivator from eviction. Short-term loans were advanced to help the farmer surmount seasonal difficulties. In the 1930's, legislation encouraged the organization of rural cooperative credit societies. In the 1930's, too, a measure of tariff protection was accorded to agricultural products and to a few industries based on local agriculture.

The economic development of the country required capital, enterprise, and planning, to drain swamps, terrace the hillsides, restore the denuded forests, develop waterpower, explore and exploit mineral resources, attract a labor force of skill and drive, and employ science to combat disease and improve agricultural and industrial processes. The British administration, however, neither undertook nor encouraged comprehensive development schemes. In fact, it tended to scrutinize sharply the plans proposed by the Jews. In the main, this was due to the "colonial" outlook of British officials, who drew on the experience of imperial administration. Industrial development might affect unfavorably a colony's usefulness as a market for home industry. Moreover, economic transformations tend to create social dislocations which, in turn, disturb imperial rule.

This imperial state of mind was reinforced by the bald fact that Palestine possessed few natural resources for industry. The bold proposals of the Jews appeared impractical and visionary. It did indeed require vision, and compelling need, too, to undertake large-scale development in Palestine, and the British, unimpelled by need, did not look beyond the immediate present.

For the Jews, however, economic development was a stern necessity. The Jewish National Home could not be built in an economically backward country. Immigration was the keystone of the projected structure, and that required absorptive capacity, which economic growth alone might supply. This urgency stimulated the dynamism and vision of the Jews, who seized upon every opportunity to plan, to build, and to create.

Planning and Guiding Agencies. A variety of agencies were fashioned to meet needs, felt and urgent or anticipated, in planning, financing, land purchase, immigrant training and absorption, labor organization, social services, education, and culture. Some were developed in Palestine; others had their origin among Jews in various countries. Several functioned independently, sometimes even with the support of non-Zionists. But the most important by far were instruments of the World Zionist movement.

The Jewish Agency. The Palestine Mandate made provision for a "Jewish Agency" to advise and cooperate in the development of the country and in other matters affecting the growth of the Jewish National Home. The Zionist Organization served as the Jewish agency until 1929, when agreement with leading non-Zionists resulted in the establishment of an enlarged body (of Zionists and non-Zionists) known as the Jewish Agency.

The Jewish Agency had no governmental powers, but its recognized status as the consultative body endowed it with considerable influence. It mobilized support for the Jewish efforts in Palestine. It negotiated with the British Government and represented the cause of the Jewish National Home before appropriate organs of the League of Nations. For the practical work of building and development in Palestine, it fashioned or utilized a network of institutions, some of which had been initiated prior to World War I. These included the Palestine Zionist Executive (or Jewish Agency Executive after 1929) and its administrative departments, which dealt with immigration, settlement on the land, the promotion of trade and industry, labor and employment, health, education and culture, statistical compilations necessary for planned development, and even meteorological observations and studies.

Financial Instruments. The main financial instruments were the Jewish National Fund and the Palestine Foundation Fund—Keren Hayesod. The former was created by the Zionist Organization in 1901 for the purpose of acquiring land as the "possession of the Jewish people." Money was raised through voluntary contributions, and the land purchased became "national" property, which was assigned on hereditary leasehold but could not be alienated as private property. Speculation in land was thus restrained, and Jewish agricultural workers were encouraged to settle on the land and work their own farms. Special provision was made that only Jewish labor be employed on National Fund land.

From its inception and until 1945-1946, the Jewish National Fund invested about 13 million pounds in Palestine. Land purchase remained its main function, but it also devoted attention to the improvement of its holdings. Through drainage, the clearance of stones, the planting of trees, and the like, considerable areas were snatched from desolation and rendered fit for settlement. The Jewish National Fund held in 1946 over 213,000 acres (865,000 dunams)—about 44% of all land owned by Jews in Palestine. These holdings were 96% rural, because the Jewish National Home placed great emphasis on agriculture. As many as 187 agricultural communities were settled on Jewish National Fund land in 1946, and there were some 50 additional workers' suburbs, collective camps, and training farms.

The Palestine Foundation Fund or Keren Hayesod was the central financial instrument of the Zionist Organization and the Jewish Agency in the building of the National Home. Organized in 1920, it succeeded in raising over £P18,000,000 (Palestine pounds) in the following 26 years, 59% of the total in the United States.

The Keren Hayesod financed a great variety of undertakings, allocating funds directly, advancing short-and-long-term loans, and setting up or supporting subsidiary companies which were able to attract additional capital. Its main efforts, however were directed to immigration and settlement. In the early years of its activities, the public services, like education and health, claimed a good part of its budget, but as the Palestine Jewish community gained in strength and assumed the burden, a higher percentage of its resources was applied to the work of immigrant absorption. Taking the period of its functioning down to 1945, approximately 65.5% of its expenditures and investments were allocated to immigration and settlement, 10.8% to education and culture, 1.0% to health and social work, 17.9% to political expenditures, security and emergency aid, and 4.8% to general administration.

Independent Bodies. The Jewish Agency and its financial affiliates were the most important instruments in the building of the National Home. In addition, other bodies contributed to the development of Jewish Palestine. Only a few can be mentioned here, and these are selected as illustrative of the widespread interest and dedication which the building of Palestine evoked among Jews of various parts of the world.

Baron Edmond de Rothschild of Paris had no faith in mass movements and he stood aloof from organized Zionism. However, his generosity was enlisted in the early 1880's, when the few Jewish settlements were in a precarious situation. He took the settlers under his tutelage, and in addition, bought large tracts of land on which new settlements were built. In 1924 the Palestine Jewish Colonization Association (PICA) took over the baron's holdings and continued his work, founding new settlements, pressing on with drainage and irrigation, and promoting industrial enterprises like salt, flour, and oil production. PICA also participated in the organization of the Palestine Electric Corporation and of other enterprises. Its major contribution, however, was agricultural settlement. By 1945 the Rothschild and PICA activities had resulted in the acquisition of about 123,000 acres (close to 500,000 dunams) and the founding or support of some 40 settlements.

Hadassah, the Women's Zionist Organization of America, concentrated its efforts on public health and medical service. It was founded in 1912 by Henrietta Szold, a magnetic and inspiring leader and organizer, whose selfless dedication welded masses of American women into an agency which worked efficiently and effectively for the advancement of the Jewish National Home. Hadassah helped raise money for the Jewish National Fund. It reached out into the broad area of social work. And during the 1930's, it became the American sponsor of Youth *Aliya,* a project which delivered thousands of Jewish children from Nazi-dominated areas and brought them up in Palestine. However, its major accomplishments were in the field of medical and health work, which will be noted elsewhere in this chapter. From 1918 to 1945, Hadassah spent in Palestine about three and one-half million pounds.

The Women's International Zionist Organization (WIZO) was organized in London in 1920 and achieved considerable success in enlisting the participation of women in Zionist work in various countries, except the United States where Hadassah was active. In Palestine its main energies were directed to the training of pioneer women in agricultural, vocational, and homemaking functions. By 1945, WIZO had expended in Palestine close to £P950,000.

Business Organizations. The agencies described above were "national" in purpose or philanthropic. A considerable contribution to the building of Palestine was made by a number of business organizations which worked with private capital independently of the Zionist bodies. The objective to help build the National Home motivated many of the leaders in these undertakings, but non-Zionist men of means participated, and the operations were conducted as business ventures. One example was the South Africa-Palestine Binyan Company, which advanced building loans on improved real estate. Another was the Palestine Corporation, an English company which played an important role in the organization of the Palestine Electric Corporation. The best illustration of this type of agency was the Palestine Economic Corporation.

The Palestine Economic Corporation was an American company, organized in the 1920's, which operated or participated in various enterprises in Palestine. Among these were banks, which financed housing for workers and advanced credits to rural and urban cooperatives and

small loans to artisans and shopkeepers. The Palestine
Economic Corporation shared in the development of a
large waste tract in the Haifa Bay area. It participated
in the establishment of the Palestine Potash Company, in
which it was the largest investor, the Palestine Electric
Corporation, the King David Hotel in Jerusalem, and
other undertakings. In all its activities, it adhered to
sound business principles but permitted only limited
profits to its shareholders.

Role of Palestine Jewry. It would be a serious error
to assume that the Jews of Palestine were passive wit-
nesses while world Jewry built the National Home, or
that the latter was reared mainly by philanthropic contributions. Palestine Jewry played an increasingly active
role during the period of the Mandate, and in retrospect
it appears that it was the predominant influence in the
actual work of building. To be sure, Palestine Jewry
must be defined not in static terms but in dynamic
terms. It was an expanding entity, with continuous accre-
tions of elements who immigrated and settled in the
country.

The administrative bodies of the Jewish Agency and
its financial instruments were staffed mainly by residents
of Palestine or by Jews who established residence there.
The operating personnel of the various economic enterprises and educational, social, and cultural institutions
were likewise in large majority Palestinians. Even in the
highest policy-making Zionist councils, the voice of the
members from Palestine carried ever greater weight.
There were also numerous agencies within Palestine
which exerted the greatest influence in the development
of the country. Among these was the Histadrut or General Federation of Jewish Labor (to be described subsequently), which profoundly affected the character of the
National Home.

The Jewish Investment in Palestine. Capital was
one of the fundamental instruments in the building of the
Jewish National Home, and this the Jews supplied in considerable amounts. Between 1917 and 1945, the Jews
brought into Palestine about £P154,000,000 which were
used for the purchase and improvement of land, the settlement of immigrants, the development of all branches

of the economy, and the support of educational, social, and cultural institutions. Of this total, 29.2% was secured by "national" and philanthropic agencies and 70.8% imported and invested as private capital in economic enterprises or brought by immigrants who settled in the country.

The sources of the contributions and investments were as varied as the human elements that sought a home in Palestine. Many were motivated by national ideals, but there were varying conceptions of the ultimate aims and of the means for their realization. The social outlook of investors, contributors, and settlers ranged from conservatism to radicalism, from proponents of a socialist commonwealth to devotees of individual enterprise. The religious orientations were equally diverse, embracing the extremes of orthodoxy and skepticism, as well as the many varieties of belief and unbelief that go by the name of moderates. And many who shared in the building of the Jewish National Home did so in response to external pressures: the settlers seeking refuge from the brutal persecution of Nazi-dominated areas or from insecurity elsewhere; the contributors and investors responding to the call to help brethren in distress. In fine, although some Jews were violently opposed to the entire venture, it would not be an exaggeration to say that the Jewish National Home was the achievement of the Jewish People, however one defines that term. And in this achievement, the planning and guiding influence was wielded by the Zionist movement and Palestine Jewry.

Growth of Jewish Population. From the early 1880's until the establishment of the State of Israel in 1948, a continuing stream of Jewish immigration flowed into Palestine. (*See Reading No. 8A.*) The volume varied from year to year, alternating between periods of concentrated or "mass" immigration and sluggish years when the flow was reduced to a trickle. However, except for the years of World War I, neither political barriers nor economic hardship could halt completely the tide of Jewish immigration.

Throughout these years, many of the immigrants were motivated by the desire to build a new national life in the old homeland, but the external pressures of anti-Semitism

played a significant role in stimulating the periodic waves
of immigration. Each wave of immigration has been
termed an *aliya*. (*See Reading No. 14.*)

In 1882, the Jewish population of Palestine was about
24,000. The Russian pogroms of 1881 set in motion the
First *Aliya,* which brought into the country some 25,000
Jews in the following two decades. The Kishenev massacre of 1903 and the failure of the Russian Revolution
of 1905 stimulated the Second *Aliya,* which continued
until World War I and resulted in the immigration of
about 40,000 Jews, principally young and nationally
motivated working people. Emigration reduced the totals
somewhat, so that by 1914, Palestine Jewry numbered
about 85,000 and constituted about 12% of the total
population of the country of about 700,000.

Turkish hostility, deportations, and epidemics during
World War I reduced the Jewish population, which stood
at about 56,000 in 1918. When the bars to immigration
were lowered in 1920, the Third *Aliya,* mainly from
Russia, brought into the country about 25,000 Jews
within three years. This was followed by the Fourth
Aliya, principally from Poland, where the Jews were
subjected to an economic boycott. During 1924-1926,
over 62,000 Jewish immigrants reached Palestine, and
nearly 20,000 more arrived during the following five
years. By 1931, the Jewish population of Palestine had
reached approximately 174,000—close to 17% of the
total population of 1,033,314.

Nazi persecution stimulated the Fifth *Aliya* of about
225,000 Jews who reached Palestine in the course of
eight years (1932-1939). At the close of 1939, conserva-
tive estimates of the Palestine Government placed the
Jewish population at about 445,000 or close to 30% of
the total population of approximately 1,500,000.

The hazards of travel and the severe restrictions of the
British authorities in Palestine discouraged immigration
during World War II. For European Jews, however, flight
was the alternative to death, and more than 54,000 found
their way into Palestine during the years 1940-1945.
Similarly, neither the turmoil of the postwar years in
Palestine nor the determination of the British to bar immigration deterred the survivors of Nazi savagery, and by
the time the British left Palestine in May, 1948, an addi-

tional 56,000 Jews had penetrated the country. When the independence of Israel was proclaimed on May 14, 1948, the Jewish population was probably about 650,000. (*See Reading No. 9A.*)

To recapitulate, when modern Jewish immigration to Palestine began in 1882, the Jews were an insignificant minority of some 24,000 souls who lived on sufferance, evinced neither national nor political consciousness, and were wanting in the means or desire for self-help. During the following sixty-six years, about 550,000 Jews, including illegal immigrants, reached Palestine. More than 60,000 Jews left the country during this period, but natural increase added considerably to the total Jewish population. By 1948, Palestine Jewry had become a self-reliant community of 650,000 imbued with national purpose, conscious of its aims, and determined to see to their realization.

Settlement on the Land and Agricultural Development. In 1882, the small Jewish population was concentrated in separate quarters in a few cities like Jerusalem, Safed, Tiberias, and Hebron. This "old Yishuv," dedicated to pious observance and study of religious lore, had struck few roots in the economy of the country and subsisted mainly in poverty on charitable collections from abroad. It was the new immigrants, after 1882, who began to transform to reality the ideal of returning to the soil. They established agricultural settlements, and although hardship and disease plagued their efforts, they persevered and held their footing. Under the British Mandate, agricultural development continued, as the Jewish public bodies directed their best efforts to settlement on the land.

With few exceptions, the Jewish holdings of land were acquired by purchase at high prices mainly from large and absentee landowners, and costly reclamation had to be undertaken to render the land fit for settlement. In 1882, Jews were in possession of less than 6,200 acres (25,000 dunams). By 1914, the total exceeded 103,000 acres (420,600 dunams), and by 1946, the Jews had acquired by purchase or concession about 446,000 acres (1,807,000 dunams).

By any standard of measurement, the Jewish holdings constituted a small fraction of the land of Palestine. The

precise size of the fraction must vary with the definition
of the country's area. Compared with the total area, it
was less than 7%. If the southland (i.e., the Negev),
then totally undeveloped, is excluded, the proportion was
about 12%. It is even more difficult to determine what
proportion of the "cultivable" area of Palestine the Jews
held, because the definition of that elusive term varied.
The British authorities regarded as cultivable the land
which was actually worked or could be worked by prevailing Arab agricultural methods. By that definition, a
great deal of the land which the Jews had bought, developed, and rendered fit for cultivation (close to 30%
of Jewish land) would have remained uncultivable. Of
the land actually under cultivation, the area worked by
Jews in 1944-1945 was approximately 9% of the total.
At that time, the Jews constituted close to one-third of
the population of Palestine.

On these meager land holdings, the Jews built the agricultural base of their National Home. From 5 agricultural settlements in 1882, with a population of about 500,
the number reached 47 in 1914, when some 12,000 Jews
(of a total Jewish population of about 85,000) were
occupied with the cultivation of grapes, oranges, and
wheat and with mixed farming, including dairy, vegetables, and poultry. The impulse to press on with land
settlement continued under the British Mandate, and by
the time the latter was terminated in May, 1948, the
number of rural settlements had increased to some 293,
with a population of about 110,000.

A comparative note will underscore the striking character of this achievement: whereas a Jewish rural population was practically non-existent in Palestine prior to
1882, two generations of colonization not only increased
the number and proportion of the total Jewish population but also created a viable balance between the rural
and the urban elements. In 1948, more than 16% of
the Jewish population of Palestine lived in rural settlements.

These figures suggest concentration of effort and speed
in rural development, but they cannot convey the intensity of zeal and spirit of dedication which inspired the
"return to the soil" movement. Nor can they conjure up
the obstacles which challenged the pioneers, the hardships

endured, the sacrifices made. To appreciate the magnitude of the achievement in agriculture, we should note that the Jews had long been divorced from the land and had occupied themselves for centuries with trade and handicrafts; that the land of Palestine posed problems of climate and disease, of deficiencies in water and fertility; that the rural Arab population was primitive and generally unfriendly. To develop Jewish agriculture, it was necessary to create the farmer and the land, the human material as well as the soil. The immigrants had to be taught how to work the land, and many of them attended preparatory training camps in their native countries before they were allowed to proceed to Palestine.

Naturally, the cost of Jewish agriculture and land settlement was high, requiring central planning, experimentation, and subsidizing of the rural settlements. The bulk of Jewish-owned land was purchased by the Jewish National Fund and by the Baron Edmond de Rothschild. Jewish enterprise devoted itself to the discovery of new sources of water and to the proper distribution and utilization of available supplies. Deeper borings and modern equipment brought about a manifold increase in the water resources of the country, and centralized irrigation works husbanded the supplies of well-watered regions for use elsewhere. In this manner, large tracts of arid land were opened to cultivation and settlement.

Much planning, experimentation and discussion accompanied the development of Jewish agriculture, with research and training playing a prominent role in its development. Experiment stations, demonstration farms, and training schools were maintained. Basic research was directed to the improvement of the soil, the selection of superior seeds, the breeding of high-grade livestock, the increase in yield, the acclimatization of new species of trees and fruit, the combatting of animal and plant diseases. Improved methods of cultivation and the use of machinery likewise contributed to the development of an agricultural economy more characteristic of the West than of the Middle East. The results of scientific agriculture were strikingly revealed in the comparative size of the average Jewish farm: in 1900, the average agricultural unit was over 36 acres; in 1945, it was less than 9 acres. The accomplishments of Jewish agriculture were indeed impressive. Beginning in the 1880's, with little beyond the untried ideal "to return to the soil," six decades of persistent national effort fashioned a solid agricultural base for the economy of Jewish Palestine. At first wholly dependent for its food supply upon Arab agriculture and imports from abroad, Palestine Jewry had contrived by 1945 to supply two-thirds of the vegetables, fruit, milk, and eggs which it consumed, and nearly one-half of the entire food supply of the Jewish population of the country. The imponderable results were perhaps even more significant. The achievement proved that Jews could become successful farmers and that barren Palestine could be restored.

Urban Development. Although left mainly to private initiative, urban and industrial development kept pace with and even surpassed that of Jewish agriculture. The growth of the Jewish city population was especially striking. Jerusalem counted less than 14,000 Jews in 1880, nearly 34,000 in 1922 (54.3% of total population), some 97,000 in 1944-1945 (61.8% of total population), and about 102,000 in 1948. Tel Aviv, founded in 1909 as a suburb of Jaffa, grew rapidly as an all-Jewish city with a population of some 1,800 in 1914, about 15,000 in 1922, 174,000 in 1945, and about 190,000 in 1948. Haifa's Jewish population of some 3,000 at the outbreak of World War I more than doubled by 1922, when the Jews constiuted about 25% of the city's population. In 1944-1945, the Jews numbered 66,000—over 55% of the inhabitants. Even Jaffa, an Arab city, with some 5,000 Jews in 1922 (15.6% of the population) saw its Jewish inhabitants increase to 34,000 by 1944-1945, when they constituted 30% of the city's population. The Jewish population of smaller towns like Tiberias likewise increased, and several rural centers expanded into towns.

Industrial Growth. Industrial development was equally marked. Before World War I, industry in the modern sense was barely known in Palestine. Immigration and the influx of capital which resulted from the promise of the Jewish National Home led to a moderate growth in industrial activity during the 1920's, but it was only after 1933 that industry became an important factor in the economy of the country. The large immigration induced by Nazi persecution included persons, especially from Germany, with industrial experience and capital, and the extensive building activities as well as expanding purchasing power provided a ready market for the numerous industrial enterprises which were established or expanded in size and equipment.

However, Palestine's industry functioned under serious handicaps even during the 1930's. In other Middle Eastern countries, such as Turkey and Iran, the state fostered the development of industry, but in Palestine, the British authorities looked upon efforts at industrialization with skepticism. And Jewish organized self-help could compensate only in part for the lack of government encouragement.

The necessity of importing raw materials increased production costs, while the demand for consumer goods attracted foreign manufactures. Protection against dumping appeared indicated, but the open-door policy of the Mandate precluded tariff protection. The riots and disturbances which became endemic after 1936, and the consequent curtailment of immigration, likewise reduced effective demand for the products of industry.

World War II witnessed a decisive growth of Palestine's industry. The sources of foreign manufactures dried up, eliminating foreign competition and leaving local markets to home industries, and war requirements encouraged Palestine's industry to expand into an important source of military supplies. Industrial personnel doubled, factories produced to capacity, enterprises multiplied, and new industries were introduced. A British authority estimated in 1943 that the Jewish share in capital investments and value of production in Palestine's industry was about 85%, while the Jewish share in industrial production for the armed forces was over 95%.

The statistical tables in Part II (*see Readings Nos. 10A and 10B*) highlight the growth of industry and provide comparative data on the economic development of Palestine. But only a study in depth could reveal the degree of mechanization in the Jewish sector of Palestine industry, the influence of specialists and experts and of a modern working class, and other aspects of advanced industrial processes. For example, industry meant predominantly handicrafts in the early 1920's, whereas in 1943, handicrafts accounted for only a fraction of the total invested capital and annual output. Professor Alfred Bonné of the Hebrew University of Jerusalem, an outstanding authority in the field, concluded that "Palestine is the only country [in the Middle East] presenting, mainly in its Jewish sector, the picture of an economy approaching that of the developed communities of the West."

Commerce and Foreign Trade. Domestic commerce, like Palestine industry, showed a rapid rate of growth, but it must be remembered that Palestine even before partition, was a small country, and total figures will hardly appear impressive, especially to American readers. For example, a comparison of Jewish wholesale trade in 1931 and 1937 shows an increase in establishments from 194 to 423; in personnel from 658 to 2,370; in capital investment from some £P515,000 to about £P2,085,000; and in sales from about £P2,345,000 to approximately £P6,674,000. During the same interval (1931 to 1937) retail establishments more than doubled; personnel increased over 2.8%; sales more than tripled; and capital investment multiplied tenfold.

In describing the expansion of the Palestine economy, we have concentrated on the Jewish sector of agriculture, industry, and commerce. Foreign trade cannot as readily be dissected on a communal basis (that is, Jewish and non-Jewish), but the foreign trade of Palestine under the British Mandate reflected the expanding economy of the Jewish National Home.

An expanding economy, especially of an underdeveloped country, requires heavy imports of capital goods for industry and agriculture. Exports develop more slowly, as production increases beyond local needs. In the case of Palestine, quantities of consumers' goods had to be imported to provide for the rapidly growing population, but it was largely the requirements of an expanding economy that accounted for the increasing volume of imports.

Foreign trade—imports and exports—is an index of the economic development of a country, and by that standard, the intensity of development of Palestine's economy exceeded the Middle Eastern countries. In the latter 1930's, imports per head of population were several times those of Iraq, Egypt, Turkey, Syria, and Lebanon, and even exports per unit of population were greater in Palestine than in the neighboring countries. Moreover, the imports and exports per head of population of Jewish Palestine were far greater than those of the country's Arabs. In fact, the index of foreign trade per unit of population, as well as other standards of measurement, placed the intensity of economic development of Jewish Palestine in a category approaching that of the industrialized states of the West. (*See Reading No. 10B.*)

During 1923-1945, imports increased eightfold, and while exports consistently lagged far behind imports, the *rate* of increase of exports was nearly twice that of imports. The balance of trade was consistently adverse or unfavorable, that is, imports exceeded exports, but the percentage of imports covered by exports rose markedly. Thus in 1923, exports were less than 29% of imports, but by 1945, fully 50% of imports were balanced by exports.

However, a trade deficit—excess of imports over exports—remained throughout the period, and it reached a peak of nearly £P20,000,000 in 1945. Such deficits are not uncommon in expanding economies, but they are frequently covered by foreign loans which impose heavy burdens of interest payments. Palestine's deficits, or adverse trade balances were covered by what economists call "invisible exports"—by capital brought in by immigrants, money spent in the country by tourists and pilgrims, remittances received from abroad, and funds collected in various countries by the Zionist agencies. The effect was that a large proportion of the goods imported into Palestine did not have to be balanced by exports, because payment was made through the "invisible exports." Thus Palestine's unfavorable *balance of trade* was counteracted by a favorable *balance of payments*.

— 5 —

DISTINCTIVE FEATURES OF THE JEWISH NATIONAL HOME

The material progress of Palestine was noteworthy rather than unique. Economic expansion was not uncommon in underdeveloped regions after World War I, and even colonial territories were astir with economic change. Jewish immigration did introduce a new population element. But if the only motivation of the immigrants had been wealth or economic betterment, a "colonial" situation might have developed. The Jews might have become plantation owners or industrial entrepreneurs, fashioning an economy based on cheap native labor and a backward social structure.

The Jewish National Home was not reared on cheap labor, native or immigrant; its architects were not dominated by the profit motive; its economy was not geared to the exploitation of natural resources for the enrichment of investors; its financial backers were not motivated by gain but by national idealism or philanthropy. The Jewish National Home was stirred by two fundamental ideals—the urge to national regeneration, and the spirit of *halutziut* or dedicated pioneering. It sought to restore a neglected and impoverished land, to create a Jewish peasantry, independent in spirit and imbued with the desire for self-help, to establish industry on the foundations of trained specialists, skilled and well-paid workers, high productivity, and modern labor relations. It experimented with forms of social organization in which cooperation rather than competition was the motivating ideal. And permeating all these efforts was the conviction that social stability and social change must rest on respect for human personality, individual freedom and democratic processes. These aims, and the measure of their realization, were the unique features of the Jewish National Home.

National Regeneration. All who subscribed to the ideal of national regeneration in Palestine sought to restore to the country a vital Jewish community. This entailed a *national* economy, with Jews settled on the land and occupied with all forms of industry and commerce, a *national* language and culture, *national* institutions, and a representative Jewish leadership.

National rebirth meant more. It meant the ingathering of the "exiles" (the *Galut*) and their spiritual regeneration. No longer would the Jew, in the words of Ben Gurion, "wander between ghetto and assimilation, between extinction and self-extinction, between escape from the world and escape from himself. . . ." Restored to the land of their ancestors, Jews would fashion their lives and their culture in accord with their heritage and with the insights of modern thought and modern science.

Halutziut. The ideal of *halutziut* (*see Reading No. 11*) was the means whereby national regeneration was to be effected. Like national rebirth, pioneering was envisaged in spiritual as well as material terms. It meant not only restoring the land and enduring the hardships of the frontier but also reclaiming the latent resources of the Jewish people. Faith, resolution, and foresight were qualities indispensable to pioneering.

Halutziut denied the arbitrary division of human beings into a ruling elite and a mass of "colorless clay of lesser mortals." Its faith endowed every person, however humble, with heroic qualities, with unplumbed spiritual reserves which could be released for creative achievement. Human liberty and equality were the elemental forces which could unlock man's dormant virtues of self-worth and self-discipline, of courage and creativeness, of the will to unity and cooperation. And *halutziut* was dedicated to service—service to the group and to what is worthy in the common cause.

These ideals and the complex of thought, hope, and faith which had their roots in the Jewish heritage—in the "inherited" values of the group—as well as in the experience of modern, European living (*see Reading No. 12*) produced the distinctive features of the Jewish National Home.

Rebirth of the Hebrew Language. The Hebrew language never faded from the consciousness of the Jews.

It ceased long ago to be the spoken tongue of the masses, but throughout the centuries, Hebrew remained the medium of prayer wherever Jews worshipped, and it persisted as a literary language, especially in poetry and in religious lore, and in part it served as a vehicle of correspondence and of personal and communal records among Jews.

The revival of Hebrew was an integral part of early Jewish nationalism in the nineteenth century, especially in eastern Europe, and when the Zionist movement directed its energies to Jewish settlement in Palestine, prodigious efforts were made to revive Hebrew as the spoken language of the Jewish settlers. These efforts were symbolized by the single-minded zeal of Eliezer Ben-Yehudah, an immigrant from Lithuania in 1881, who devoted his life to the cause.

The primary aim of the Hebrew movement was reunion with the spiritual influence of the ancient past, but the ideal had great practical value as well, for Hebrew served as a profound unifying force. The settlers brought with them a great variety of languages, and schools maintained by European philanthropic societies employed French, German, or English as the language of instruction. If fragmentation was to be avoided, a common language was indispensable, and Hebrew alone claimed at least the historical loyalty of all Jews.

The proponents of Hebrew concentrated their best efforts upon the schools, and strong exception was taken to the use of any language other than Hebrew as the medium of instruction. Opposition extended even to Yiddish, the vernacular spoken by the masses of East European Jews. Success was most marked in the Zionist agricultural settlements, and by the time of World War I, Hebrew was the medium of instruction in practically all preschool and elementary grades in the settlements, and even in a number of city schools, including important secondary schools and a teacher-training agency. It has been estimated that by 1914, Hebrew was the vernacular of nearly 54% of all boys aged two to fourteen, and that about 40% of all Jews above one year of age spoke the language.

Throughout the period of the Mandate, the Hebraizing of Jewish Palestine was pressed with embattled zeal. Hebrew became *the* medium or *a* medium of instruction in all but a small fraction of the Jewish schools. In the selection of labor immigrants, preference was given to applicants with some knowledge of the language. The rural settlements became entirely Hebrew-speaking, as the generation reared in the schools reached maturity. In the cities and towns, various languages were spoken by adults, but the children quickly became unilingual and affected the speech of parents. Jewish agencies and institutions employed Hebrew. It was the language of the daily press, of periodical literature and publications, of the theater and cinema, of public events. By the 1940's, the tone and color of Jewish Palestine were unmistakably Hebrew.

The census of November, 1948, after the Mandate had come to an end, revealed the full scope of the achievement. Over 75% of all Jews above two years of age spoke Hebrew, and it was the language of over 93% of all children aged two to fourteen. (*See Reading No. 13.*)

In retrospect the achievement appears startling. To be sure, the schools were a powerful assimilating agent, but they might have proved less than adequate, had not the newcomers been psychologically attuned to the new influence. The immigrants were fleeing from inhospitable lands, from "exile" that was real and poignant, and Palestine was more than a haven of refuge. To the vast majority, it was the ancestral homeland to which they were returning, and the very idea of returning predisposed them to change. They were to share in the process of national regeneration. The link with the ancient past was to be refastened; the severed members of the nation were to be rejoined; and a new breath, a new spirit, as in the prophecy of old, was to fashion a new national life. In national regeneration, the influence of language is profoundly potent, for it is more than a means of communication. It is a symbol of unity, an index of continuity, a reflection of the genius of a people. If the revival of the Hebrew language was a latter-day miracle, it was these imponderables that served as the talisman.

Education. Immigrant populations in frontier areas do not, as a rule, devote themselves to education and culture. Material needs and defense claim available energies, and only after a time lag, when security and sustenance are less precarious, do these spiritual agencies arise. In

Jewish Palestine, education and culture were primary considerations from the very outset. In part, this was conditioned by the motivations of national regeneration, but it cannot be fully explained without reference to the Jewish heritage.

Study, learning, and teaching have ranked high in the beliefs and practices of traditional Judaism since time immemorial. The Bible commands that the word of God be taught to children and adults, and schools are known to have functioned in ancient Palestine at least as early as two thousand years ago. The destruction of Jerusalem and its Temple and the dispersion of the Jews called for even greater emphasis upon learning, because the loss of the homeland and the end of the sacrificial cult made Judaism entirely dependent on Torah, the written and oral law and lore. Small wonder that Jews were warned to shun settlements without facilities for education.

Study of Torah was not just a means of acquiring knowledge or an instrument for preferment. It was an act of faith; indeed, it was regarded as a form of worship, a means of communion with God. It claimed the best minds of Jews through the centuries. It was a central factor in determining status in Jewish communities. In Jewish eyes, at least, learning symbolized the image of the good Jew.

This faith in education was part of the heritage which the Jewish immigrants brought to Palestine. Jewish settlements without schools would therefore have been incongruous under any circumstances; in the atmosphere of national revival, it was unthinkable. Thus the school accompanied the settler in town and village, and education became an integral part of the Jewish National Home.

Until the British conquest of Palestine, Jewish schools functioned as private institutions independent of government authority, and even the regime of the Mandate was content to allow wide autonomy to Jewish education. Various agencies sponsored and maintained Jewish schools, and there were wide differences in curricula, in national and religious orientation, and even in language of instruction.

In 1914, a Board of Education was established to coordinate and direct the Jewish national schools in which Hebrew was the language of instruction, and after World

War I this Hebrew public school system rapidly became the predominant factor in Jewish education. In 1925-1926, the Board of Education administered 177 of the 255 Jewish schools and 64% of the Jewish school children; in 1944-1945, it accounted for 651 of the 965 Jewish schools and 75.9% of the children. Until 1933, the Zionist Organization or the Jewish Agency was the supreme authority to whom the Board of Education was responsible and from whom it received its basic financial support. In that year, authority and responsibility were transferred to the National Council (Vaad Leumi) of the Jews of Palestine.

The total effort in Jewish education (including that of the Board of Education and of the independent schools) was most impressive. Enrolments in all types of Jewish schools grew from 26,849 in 1925-1926, to 61,173 in 1935-1936, and to 105,747 in 1944-1945. The number of teachers kept pace with enrolments, increasing from 1,145 in 1925-1926, to 2,867 in 1935-1936, and to 5,388 in 1944-1945. Expenditures, too, mounted in proportion, rising from estimated totals of about £P 300,000 in 1925-1926, to £P 850,000 in 1935-1936, and to £P2,-700,000 in 1944-1945.

It must be underscored that the far-flung Jewish educational efforts were voluntary and enjoyed a minimum of government encouragement or assistance. There was no compulsory education under the Mandate even for elementary schooling. The education department of the government did establish schools, but it regarded Arab needs as paramount, and the "government schools" developed as the Arab public school system, with Arabic as the medium of instruction. However, the government did not interfere with the content and orientation of Jewish education, a matter of vital significance to the Jews. The government set minimum requirements and exercised the right of inspection, but otherwise educational autonomy remained undisturbed.

One might be tempted to conclude that the bounty of world Jewry enabled Palestine's Jews to enjoy a luxury type of education they could ill afford. This might have validity if one disregarded the vital concern of world Jewry as an asset—material as well as spiritual—of the National Home. And even then, the conclusion would be

true only in part, because Palestine Jewry did assume the
burden of providing proper education for its youth, even
though this entailed serious sacrifices.

Close study of the financing of the Hebrew public
school system, which included an increasing majority of
the Jewish school population, and for which material is
available, reveals that a rapidly rising proportion of
school costs were borne by Palestine's Jews. In 1918-
1919, the latter supplied only about 11% of the budget,
but the figure rose quickly: it was nearly 41% in 1925-
1926; over 80% in 1935-1936; and 83.4% in 1944-1945.
In the latter year, the Jewish Agency covered only 8%
of the budget; another 8.6% was supplied by the government from tax funds; the remainder of the costs was met
by tuition fees paid by parents, allotments from local
communities and the like.

Technical and Adult Education. In addition to general education, considerable attention was given to technical training. Numerous special schools or classes were
established for instruction in agriculture, and a number
of technical and trade schools provided vocational training.

Adult or extension education was especially widespread.
Evening courses were given in towns, villages and settlements. Lectures were well attended and the subjects
ranged from literature and the arts to social theory and
questions of the day. Group visits to historic places made
the past live again, and, incidentally, spread knowledge
of nature and of Palestine geography. Reading rooms
made books and newspapers available to workers even in
remote and isolated settlements.

Higher Education. No single act symbolizes better
the unique qualities of the Jewish National Home than
the building of the Hebrew University. Therein the almost
romantic faith in education—and its vindication—are
concretized. The University exemplifies the realistic potential of lofty visions, the driving power of faith in an
ideal, the basic truth of Herzl's inspired precept: "If you
will it, it is no legend."

The idea of a Jewish university in Palestine was
broached in the early 1880's, when the first halting steps
were being taken to settle Jews there. When World War
I broke out and threatened to tear to shreds the frail

fabric of Jewish Palestine, concrete steps had been taken to further the realization of the project: some funds had been subscribed and a site had been acquired on the ridge of bleak but commanding Mount Scopus.

In July, 1918, southern Palestine had been cleared of the Turks, but the British hold on the country was still precarious. The Jewish fugitives who had been driven into exile had not yet returned, and the National Home was little more than a hope and a half-promise. At that moment, Chaim Weizmann chose to "found" the Hebrew University. Within the hearing of gunshot, twelve foundation stones were sunk into the crest of Mount Scopus—an act that was at once paradox and symbol: paradox because the realities of population and the material underpinning of the National Home were still wanting; symbol of a deeply rooted conviction that schools and learning are a shield against disintegration and a reservoir of courage and energy wherewith a future can be fashioned. Stirred by this episode, the British conqueror of Palestine called it "an act of faith in Palestine."

The University was opened officially in April, 1925. During the first few years the University was a research institution exclusively, but in 1928 provision was made also for course instruction leading initially to the master's degree. The Ph.D. was first conferred in 1936. The student body multiplied rapidly in the 1930's and reached approximately 1,000 in 1946-1947. When the British Mandate came to an end, the Hebrew University ranked among the great centers of learning of the world and the foremost seat of scholarship in the Middle East.

Higher education in the field of technology centered in the Hebrew Technical College of Haifa (generally known as the Technion). Officially opened in 1925, it grew rapidly during the 1930's, and in 1944-1945, a total of 391 students received instruction in the various branches of engineering, in architecture, and in nautical science. All studies were conducted in Hebrew. This period also witnessed the initial steps in the development of what later came to be known as the Weizmann Institute of Science.

Hebrew Culture. Variety and intensity marked the Jewish cultural life of Palestine. An art school, founded in 1906, was reorganized in 1935 as the "New Bezalel"

in which arts and crafts were taught in Hebrew. A number of painters of note settled in Palestine, and their
works were exhibited in New York and Paris as well as in
Palestine. Music was cultivated, and by 1936 a permanent
symphony orchestra, founded by Hubermann was able to
perform under the baton of Toscanini.

The theater achieved high artistic level in Palestine. The
national theater, Habima, founded in 1929, performed
regularly in Tel Aviv and went often on tour to other
towns and even to agricultural settlements. All performances were in Hebrew, with a repertoire of Jewish historical plays and translations of classical drama, notably
Shakespeare.

Ohel was a workers' theater of high merit. Its plays
were oriented toward social and economic problems, but
it performed also classical and biblical dramas. Specialized dramatic companies, among them a children's theater
and one that satirized the new life in Palestine, were likewise popular, for the zealous builders of the National
Home preserved a sense of humor. All of the theatrical
groups were cooperative undertakings, and they were in
the main self-supporting.

The relatively small Jewish population of Palestine
supported in the middle 1940's seven daily newspapers
(six in Hebrew and one in English) and a score or more
of periodicals devoted to literature, art, economics, law,
youth, etc. Books, too, were published and read in relatively large numbers. In 1946, about 1,000 titles appeared
—one book per 600 population! These included translations as well as original works in fiction, poetry, and
scholarship.

Health and Welfare. Under Turkish rule, health
conditions in Palestine were primitive. Human neglect had
converted large areas into malaria-breeding swamps, and
general lack of sanitation made rampant other diseases.
Therefore, the Jewish settlers, and the agencies which supported them, were obliged to include health measures and
medical services as integral parts of the work of settlement. Still, many a pioneer of the early period paid with
his life for his national zeal.

The British brought to the country modern and com-
petent health services, but their efforts were limited to the
minimum essentials of a colonial territory. The govern-

ment's department of health performed the usual functions of registration, quarantine, inspection, and control of infectious diseases. Since Jews and Christians maintained hospital services, the government conducted a limited number of hospitals and infant-care centers in Arab areas and in the towns. Some antimalaria work—drainage and medical treatment—was likewise done. However, the total effort and achievement of the British authorities was not materially different from the health work done in neighboring countries, like Iraq and Syria. Government services, therefore, did not account for the wide ranging and superior health work which made Palestine a unique health oasis in the disease-ridden Middle East. In some measure, this was due to Christian missionary groups who maintained hospitals, dispensaries, and clinics in the Holy Land. But it was Jewish efforts that were mainly responsible for the medical and health progress of Palestine.

The major influence for health in the Jewish National Home was Hadassah, the Women's Zionist Organization of America. Its first efforts were made before World War I, but its great potential became evident immediately after the war when, in August, 1918, it dispatched to Palestine a medical unit of forty-five physicians, nurses, sanitation and other health workers. This unit took over existing Jewish hospitals, established new ones, opened clinics and child-welfare stations in the settlements, and organized sanitary services wherever needed. The arrival of immigrants opened new fields of service in labor camps and new settlements.

In 1921, the medical unit became the Hadassah Medical Organization, a permanent body which extended its services as dictated by the needs of the expanding National Home. Some of its responsibilities were gradually transferred to local communities, as the Yishuv (Palestine Jewry) gained in strength and organization. Hadassah, however, remained pre-eminent in health work, serving numerous centers and maintaining a magnificent hospital on Mount Scopus. A nurses' training school, established in 1918 by Henrietta Szold, was continued and developed into an institution of high merit. Hadassah operated a modern health center in Jerusalem which did preventive health work in orthopedics, nutrition, and sex and mental hygiene, and also housed a pasteurization plant. Other activities of Hadassah included a hospital for tubercular diseases in Safed, a network of child-welfare stations, school luncheons, and playgrounds. Antimalaria work likewise ranked high in Hadassah's program, as did efforts to combat trachoma and tuberculosis and general medical and health research. In this work, and especially in research and in the war on disease, the Hebrew University rendered distinguished service in cooperation with Hadassah.

The most important local health organization in Jewish Palestine was Kupat Holim, the Sick Benefit Fund of the Histadrut, which maintained in 1945 in various towns and villages 5 hospitals, 5 convalescent homes, and 278 medical and dental clinics, x-ray institutes, and infant welfare stations. This agency was primarily concerned with workers' needs, and the excellent health conditions in the workers' settlements were the result of its efforts.

Kupat Holim was a cooperative welfare agency rather than merely a health organization. Established in 1911, with an initial membership of 150, it grew to over 12,000 in 1925, nearly 54,000 ten years later, and over 120,000 in 1945. If the dependents are included, Kupat Holim served in 1945 a total of 272,321 persons—about 46% of the Jewish population of the country at that time.

This voluntary agency performed the functions of health insurance, often administered by governments. The fund was composed of contributions from workers and employers, and the benefits to members and their families consisted of hospital and medical services, medicines, convalescent facilities, maternity aid, and sickness benefit allowances. Thus, regardless of the lack of compulsory health insurance in Palestine, a large proportion of the Jewish population was able to enjoy this service of the welfare state through voluntary cooperation. And there were several additional smaller mutual aid associations which provided health insurance for other elements in the Jewish population.

The expenditures of Kupat Holim grew from less than £P 42,000 in 1925 to over £P 1,493,000 in 1945. And the sources of these funds confirm the significant fact that Palestine Jewry gradually assumed financial responsibility for its local needs. At the close of the 1920's, nearly half of the budget was met by the members and by workers' cooperatives; another third was supplied by employers' contributions and patients' fees; and the remainder was covered by subsidies from Zionist funds. By the latter 1930's, however, the workers supplied over four-fifths of the budget, and the employers nearly one-fifth.

We have characterized the Jewish health and welfare services as a distinctive feature of the Jewish National Home. The term unique might have been equally applicable, because colonial territories rarely enjoy such high standards of medical care. Mere reference to the health budget of the Palestine government and comparison with Jewish expenditures will underscore this point. As early as 1925, when the Jews constituted less than 15% of the total population of Palestine, they spent on health considerably more than twice the sum allocated by the government for that purpose. And in 1945 the comparative figures were even more striking: although less than one-third the population of the country, the Jews spent on health and welfare more than three times the health budget of the government; and Kupat Holim alone, then almost entirely supported by Palestine Jewry, had a budget more than twice that of the health department of the government. The per capita expenditures on health reveal in a flash the Jews' preoccupation with health: in 1945, they spent £P 4.1 per head of Jewish population, while the government's figure was £P 0.4 per head of total population. To be sure, the government made grants-in-aid to Jewish health institutions, but these were insignificant— £P 47,000 out of its health budget of £P 731,000 in 1945. Percentagewise, the government's contribution was 2% of Jewish expenditures, and 6.4% of its health budget, when the Jewish population was over 30% of the total population.

The results of Jewish health work are reflected in the vital statistics of Palestine under the Mandate. The Jewish death rate showed an annual average of 13.70 per thousand during 1922-1925, and 8.08 per thousand during 1936-1940—figures which compared favorably with those of the most advanced countries. For Palestine as a whole, including the Jews, the coresponding figures were 23.82 per thousand during 1922-1925, and 16.48 during 1936-

1940. And for the Moslem population of Palestine, the death rate averaged 26.93 per thousand during 1922-1925, and 21.13 per thousand during 1936-1940.

The decline in infant mortality was even more marked. In 1925, infant mortality per thousand of live births stood at 189.05 for Palestine as a whole; by 1945 it had fallen to 79.9 per thousand. By religious communities, the rates of infant mortality were as follows: for the Jews—132.11 infant deaths per thousand in 1925, and 35.8 per thousand in 1945; for the Christians—162.41 per thousand in 1925, and 70.6 per thousand in 1945; for the Moslems—200.85 per thousand in 1925, and 93.9 per thousand in 1945.

Finally, we must note that Jewish health measures had a far wider influence in the country than mere figures can portray. Serving the settled areas, the government and the missionary agencies barely touched the disease-infested regions which were all but uninhabitable. The health work of the Jews was dynamic. In addition to the care of the settled Jewish population, new zones were penetrated, the malaria plague fought and mastered, and additional land rendered fit for human habitation.

Social Idealism. We have said above that the ideals of national regeneration and *Halutziut* (or pioneering) were basically responsible for the distinctive features of the Jewish National Home. These ideals help explain the revival of the Hebrew language, the devotion to education, the passion for Hebrew culture and, in part, also the concentrated attention upon health and welfare. Reference has also been made to the "inherited" values of the Jews (*see Reading No. 12*) as a source of social idealism which inspired many of the devotees of the Jewish National Home. However, the emphasis on the religious and social ideals of the Jewish heritage calls for a word of caution. Only a visionary or a sectarian with well-adjusted blinkers would suggest that these ideals governed in every detail the daily life of Jews in any age, or that principle motivated all immigrants to Palestine, or that the Jewish National Home was a Utopia. Ideals in any culture or society are not necessarily identical with the functioning realities of conduct, status, and relationship. When we say that American democracy rests on freedom and equality, it does not mean that racial and religious discrimination are non-existent or that freedom to differ is everywhere and at all times respected. An ideal is a standard of excellence toward which we strive, a societal or individual desideratum, a model against which we measure norms of conduct and patterns of status, a principle which enables us to determine success or failure in human relationships. Thus conceived, social idealism unquestionably inspired the Jewish National Home.

The Idealization of Labor. It has been noted that an aura of idealism attended the return of Jews to Palestine and the building of the National Home. Immigration to Palestine was *Aliya*—an "ascent" involving spiritual "reaching up" (*see Reading No. 14*) as well as the physical fact of "going up" into a mountainous country. The preferred imigrant was a *Halutz,* at once pioneer and vanguard, who sought not only to build a home for himself but also to help lay the foundations for a new national life. His task or mission required preparation (*hachsharah*)—spiritual orientation in the Hebrew language and national goals as well as training for work in a new land. And settlement in Palestine, at its best, meant cultivation of the soil—back to the land and to nature.

The back-to-the-land movement became identified with national regeneration. It meant return to Palestine, the abandonment of the "artificial" life of the city, physical and spiritual intimacy with nature and, above all, cultivation of the soil. Work on the land was not just a means of earning a livelihood: it was "ennobled and 'sanctified' in Palestine" as "the essential basis of the Jewish National Home." (*See Reading No. 15.*) Through agricultural and reclamation work, the land was to be redeemed, the people were to strike roots in the soil, Jewish economic life was to be "normalized" and the basis provided for a just and stable community.

Concentrated in trade, industry, and the professions, the Jews were affected both by the fact of their economic dependence upon an often hostile majority and by the ideology which stigmatized middle-class occupations as socially less useful. They came to regard their distribution in the European economy as abnormal and were determined not to reproduce that situation in Palestine. In the

National Home, Jews were to share in all branches of economic life, with special emphasis upon "primary" economic pursuits, notably agriculture.

The central ideal in this social ferment was manual labor—self-labor and toil. Through labor, the land was to be recovered, and the human material, too, was to be reclaimed through manual work. Many of the early settlers who came of middle-class families and were well educated, preferred the hard life in the agricultural settlements to professional or business careers. This was especially true of the immigrants of the Second *Aliya* who launched an uncompromising struggle for the "conquest of labor" and the "conquest of watching," the latter referring to the dangerous work of guarding the settlements against thievery and plunder. As the National Home grew, the campaign for self-labor extended to city work—to hauling and carting, toil on the docks, in the workshops and quarries, and in construction. The highest ideal, however, was to work on the land, and the greatest merit attached to "black labor," that is, the back-breaking toil of reclaiming wasteland and draining the infested swamps which often menaced health and life.

The Collective and Cooperative Settlements. The current of social idealism in the Jewish National Home was fed by various streams of thought, and it sustained a variety of institutional patterns. But all of the latter were molded by these guiding principles: that everyone should live by his own labor; that no man should become an instrument for the profit of another; that cooperation and mutual aid were the best safeguards of freedom and equality. The most far-reaching efforts to realize these objectives were the novel forms of group living evolved in the collective and cooperative settlements. However, while the collective settlements were animated by socialistic ideals, practical considerations were determining factors both in their development and in the support they received from the non-socialist majority of the Zionist movement.

The early Jewish settlers lacked the means as well as the agricultural experience to undertake farming without assistance. Since subsidies and training were essential, group efforts yielded better results than those of isolated individuals. The costs of housing and equipment, of food and its preparation, were reduced. The inexperienced could work under the guidance of the better trained, and individual failure and disappointment did not lead to the abandonment of farms. Moreover, group life sustained both the morale and the subsistence level of Jewish workers when the competition of cheap Arab labor tended to undermine both. All this was foreseen, and experiments in cooperative farming were actually undertaken before the collectives emerged.

A rich and colorful terminology was evolved to identify the various forms of cooperative settlement in Palestine. The *kvutzah* (plural, *kvutzot*) and the *kibbutz* (plural, *kibbutzim*) were the prototypes of collective settlements in the Jewish National Home. The *kvutzah* developed as a commune in which property and income, production and distribution were socialized. Each member contributed his labor and each received, not wages, but the necessities and small luxuries from the pooled earnings of the group. The atmosphere was that of a family whose members worked together and shared in the joys and cares of a common endeavor. Children enjoyed especially favored treatment in housing, food, and medical care. As a rule, the younger children lived in quarters separate from the parents and under the care of nurses and teachers. However, the filial bond was not weakened thereby.

The land of the *kvutzah* was generally leased from the Jewish National Fund and no hired labor even of Jews was permitted. The supreme authority of the commune was the General Assembly of its members, which selected appropriate governing committees. Women enjoyed full equality with men, sharing authority as well as the tasks of the community.

The word *kibbutz* developed to identify a variant type of collective, especially in its preparatory stage of organization. As a rule, the *kvutzah* was a self-contained group in which all the members lived and worked together. Some collectives, however, were formed before settlement on the land could be achieved, or when only a fraction of the membership could be settled. Such a collective was designated a *kibbutz*. An advance guard would till the soil and prepare the future home of the entire group, while the remainder worked at trades in the cities and remitted the savings to the "home" unit. Such a *kibbutz* was a collective which embraced urban workers as well as agricultural settlers who cooperated in building the future home on the land.

Another type of *kibbutz* consisted of a group formed on the outskirts of a settlement of privately owned farms. The members lived together on land assigned to them, but when the land could not support the entire group, a portion worked for wages on neighboring farms and turned over their earnings to the common treasury.

Once established on the land, the communal norms of conduct and relationships within the *kibbutz* were substantially like those of the *kvutzah*. The basic ideals of voluntary membership and democratic procedures, of self-labor especially on the land, of equality of the sexes, and of common ownership and shared production and distribution were accepted in both. By the logic of definition, a settled *kibbutz* should therefore have become a *kvutzah*. However, in many instances, the term *kibbutz* was retained even after the entire group lived and worked on the collective farm. In practice, then, while some collectives were known by the name of *kibbutz* and others by that of *kvutzah*, the terms came to be used interchangeably as descriptive of the collective community. And "*kibbutz*" became the generic expression for the collective movement.

The first collective, Dagania, was established in the upper Jordan valley in 1909. By 1914 there were four such settlements with a combined population of 180. But the movement spread rapidly during the period of the Mandate, and in 1945, no less than 140 *kibbutzim* and *kvutzot* were in existence, with an adult membership of 17,000. The total population of these collectives, including children, relatives, dependents, candidates, and training groups, exceeded 40,000.

The fundamental problem of freedom *versus* security was reflected in the development of differing forms of cooperative agricultural settlements. The all-pervasive communal life of the collectives provided a maximum of security, at the sacrifice, however, of personal freedom— freedom to enjoy the intimacy and privacy of the family circle, to select one's work, to satisfy personal preference in luxuries. There were men and women who favored cooperation but preferred a greater measure of personal liberty, even if that entailed some loss in security. Such people fashioned new forms of cooperative agricultural settlements which combined in varying degrees features of individualism and collectivism. The cooperative (as distinct from the collective) settlements included three main types: the smallholders' settlement (*moshav*); the workers' smallholders' settlement (*moshav ovdim*); and the collective smallholders' settlement (*moshav shitufi*).

The Cooperative Movement in Industry, Trade and Services: The cooperative movement was not limited to the agricultural settlements but extended to urban industries, trade and services as well. Modern cooperatives made their first appearance prior to 1914, when the Jewish population was small, and they expanded rapidly with the growth of population under the British Mandate until they permeated the entire economy of the Jewish National Home. In 1945, when the Jews numbered less than 600,000, they maintained about 1,000 cooperative societies, with a combined membership of some 350,000 and total resources in excess of £P 32,000,000.

Marketing cooperatives were among the first to be organized in Jewish Palestine. The most successful was Tnuvah, which concerned itself primarily with the domestic sale of produce of the agricultural settlements affiliated with the General Federation of Jewish Labor, whose agency it was. In 1945, Tnuvah marketed over one-half of the produce of Jewish agriculture—over 70% of the produce which was sold through organized channels.

The most succesful urban cooperatives were in the field of motorized transportation, both local and inter-urban. In 1945, the bulk of Jewish motorized transportation was organized cooperatively. Consumer cooperatives developed slowly, and in 1945 there were fewer than 140 local societies, with a combined membership of some 25,000 and total resources of about three-quarters of a million Palestine pounds. Most of the local consumer societies were affiliated with Hamashbir, the central agency for workers' consumer cooperation. The societies were successful in the villages, but far less so in the cities, where privately owned trade flourished. In the villages they supplied the farmers with manufactured and imported goods and received in return their produce for delivery to Tnuvah.

Industrial producers' cooperatives were neither numerous nor widespread. In 1945, small numbers were functioning in metal and woodwork production, wearing apparel, building materials, printing, and other crafts. However, a unique form of contracting cooperatives exerted a strong influence on the economy of Palestine. They were concerned primarily with home building and highway construction but they branched out into industrial production as well. They were agencies of the General Federation of Jewish Labor and will be described presently.

Home-building cooperatives were especially popular. A country of immigration, Jewish Palestine always suffered from a shortage of housing, and neither the government nor the municipalities occupied themselves with the problem. Private initiative supplied the major portion of the capital for construction, but cooperative societies played an important role.

Water supply and irrigation were vital in Palestine, and the digging of wells and modern irrigation works were costly. Holdings, on the other hand were small, and the owners, whether communities or individuals, could neither afford to sustain such operations, nor did they require, in many instances, more than a fraction of the capacity of a well. Cooperative irrigation societies therefore developed and spread rapidly. In 1945, some 69 were functioning, of which Mekorot was best known. This cooperative was mainly concerned with supplying water to the settlements in the western part of the Plain of Esdraelon from sources around Haifa.

Finally, cooperation was notable in the field of credit and banking and, to a lesser extent, in insurance. Some 93 cooperative credit and thrift societies were in business in 1945, with more than 86,000 members and over £P 10,000,000 in total resources.

The urban cooperatives were concerned with common production and not with common living, and a person's cooperative affiliation could be partial rather than all-embracing. One could be a member of a transportation cooperative without obligation to join a housing or consumer cooperative. Often the cooperative was really a facility, as when dwellings were built by a cooperative and owned privately by the purchasers. In short, the urban cooperative movement provided greater security in employment and often higher earnings. Above all, it tended to reduce costs and facilitate the growth of the Jewish National Home.

Although the cooperative movement affected and, in a measure, involved all of Jewish Palestine, it was essentially a product of the same forces which fashioned the Jewish labor movement. Some labor elements championed cooperation as an ideal, as the antithesis to competition. They saw in the network of cooperatives the beginnings of a new society in which private trade and industry would disappear, and with them the profit motive and "exploitation."

However, the development of the cooperatives, and their actual functioning, warrant the conclusion that the cooperative commonwealth was a secondary consideration. The primary purpose of all Jewish efforts in Palestine, the cooperatives included, was the building of the Jewish National Home. And in the process of building, abstract ideals and preconceived doctrines yielded to the necessities of promoting immigration and facilitating land settlement and urban development in order to absorb the newcomers. The cooperative movement was for some persons an end, a feature of the ideal society of the future. But more emphatically, it was a means—an effective method of building the Jewish National Home.

The General Federation of Jewish Labor (Histadrut). The Histadrut was by far the most important, but not the only Jewish labor organization in Palestine. An organization of religious workers (Hapoel Hamizrahi), formed shortly after the Histadrut, functioned independently, although often in close cooperation with the Histadrut. In the 1930's, the extreme nationalists, known as the Revisionists, set up an independent National Federation of Labor. Separate unions of Oriental Jews appeared at times, and the extreme orthodox wing of Palestine Jewry (Agudat Israel) set up its own labor organization. These fragments, however, were obscured by the Histadrut, which included (after 1930) close to three-quarters of all the Jewish workers of the country.

The Histadrut was organized toward the end of 1920, with an initial membership of 4,400. It grew rapidly, doubling its membership by 1925, when it embraced some 53% of all gainfully employed Jews in Palestine. In 1930, as much as 74% of all Jewish workers were members of the Histadrut (20,200 members of a total of 27,300 workers), and this proportion was maintained, with minor fluctuations, for the remainder of the period of the Mandate. In 1945, the Histadrut membership (exclusive of the wives of workers) was 113,600 out of the 152,000 of gainfully employed Jews (74%). The total Jewish population was then under 600,000.

The Histadrut was one of the most unique of the institutions developed in the Jewish National Home. As a central organization of labor, it aimed to further the interests of the working class; but its purposes and functions were national in scope and orientation. As a federation of trade unions, it was concerned with wages, hours, and working conditions. However, the Histadrut transcended its member unions, and its manifold activities went far beyond the normal range of labor agencies. In membership and services, in structure and purposes, it represented a most unusual type of labor organization.

Membership in the Histadrut was open to all workers who lived by their own labor. Manual labor was, of course, idealized in Histadrut circles, but the term "worker" was not limited to wage-earners engaged in physical labor. The members of the workers' agricultural settlements—farmers, and certainly not wage-earners—were welcome in the Histadrut, and in 1945, they composed 20% of the membership of the organization. Similarly, "mental workers" were included: 10.3% of the membership consisted of salaried clerks and office workers in 1945; and 4.4% were members of the liberal professions—teachers, doctors, lawyers, technicians, and the like. The Histadrut was thus a labor organization which embraced industrial and farm workers, the skilled and unskilled, wage-earners, cooperative farmers, white-collar workers, and members of the liberal professions.

The manifold functions performed by the Histadrut may be grouped under three headings, namely, (1) trade-union and welfare activities; (2) cooperative economic enterprises, and (3) educational, cultural, and social services.

The trade-union activities included the usual efforts connected with organizing, bargaining, and labor conflicts. The trade-union objectives and, to a notable extent, the achievements of Jewish labor in Palestine tended to approximate those of the industrially advanced states of the West. The Histadrut sought to regulate employment by written or oral agreements based on collective bargaining. It maintained labor exchanges and pressed employers to hire workers through those agencies. It resisted the arbitrary discharge of workers and won acceptance of the principle of separation allowances. In a good proportion of the establishments, annual vacations were secured, as well as insurance against industrial accidents and contributions to the Sick Benefit Fund. The advanced character of Jewish labor relations in Palestine is perhaps best illustrated by the fact that the Histadrut and the Palestine Jewish Manufacturers Association were able to arrange by mutual agreement for cost-of-living allowances in 1939, several years before the Palestine government began to concern itself with this matter.

The Histadrut sought also through self-help to alleviate the effects of insecurity resulting from illness, unemployment, and old age. The Sick Benefit Fund which has been described above (page 58) received some assistance from employers and from the Palestine government (14.7% and 0.6% respectively of total income in 1945). Other funds received no employers' contributions or government grants-in-aid, and were maintained by 1945 almost entirely from workers' contributions. An unemployment fund was used as a reserve for periods of depression, especially for the creation or promotion of useful public works. An old-age and survivor fund and a disability fund provided assistance for invalids, for widows and orphans, and for the aged.

The Histadrut not only guarded the interests of workers in the economic life of the country but it was also involved directly in the ownership and management of units of production, marketing, transportation, banking, and other services. These activities were cooperative ventures in which the Histadrut served either as the central agency of cooperating units or as the direct employer of labor and producer of goods and services. In other words, the Histadrut was an association of cooperatives as well as a labor federation.

Control over the economic enterprises was lodged in a body which was co-extensive with the Histadrut, the members of the one being automatically members of the other. This was the Workers Association (Hevrat Ovdim), organized in 1924 as a holding company to supervise the economic activities. Among the subsidiaries of the Workers Association were many of the cooperatives mentioned above, including Tnuvah, the agricultural marketing cooperative, and the Central Consumers' Co-operative (Hamashbir).

Another type of economic agency was Solel Boneh, a contracting cooperative, which began with road building and house construction. Subsequently it entered the industrial field, acquiring stone quarries and manufacturing building materials and accessories, such as bricks, glass, plumbing, and the like. In 1944, it employed 6,500 workers and had a turnover of £P 4,130,000. A similar but smaller subsidiary (Yakhin) undertook the cultivation and management of citrus plantations on a contractual basis.

The Workers' Bank was the most important financial instrument of the Histadrut. Founded in 1921, it became an important source of credit for the collective farms, urban cooperatives, contracting agencies and other units of the network of labor cooperatives. In 1944, its capital amounted to £P 448,000, deposits totaled over two and three-quarter million Palestine pounds, and loans came close to one and one-half millions.

The Histadrut was also engaged in far-reaching educational and cultural activities. Through its Central Bureau of Education, it conducted schools which had autonomous status within the Hebrew school system of the country. Beginning in 1921 with one school of 19 pupils, the number increased rapidly so that by 1935-1936, there were 125 schools, 288 teachers, and 6,217 pupils. In 1944-1945, the Histadrut operated 267 schools with 1,009 teachers and 18,399 pupils. These figures represented 41% of the schools of the Hebrew school system, 27% of the teachers, and 22.9% of the pupils. The schools were located mainly in the workers' agricultural settlements, and the labor ideals of the Histadrut figured prominently in the course of studies.

Adult education and culture were sponsored by the Cultural Committee of the Histadrut in cooperation with the local Labor Councils. Reading rooms and clubs were established, even in remote settlements. In cities, towns, and agricultural villages, classes and lectures were arranged on various subjects, ranging from the Bible to modern literature, and from popular science to social and political problems of the day. Special attention was devoted to recent immigrants, who were taught the Hebrew language and labor ideals. Familiarity with the country and with Jewish achievements in Palestine was promoted through illustrated lectures and conducted tours and hikes.

The arts were represented by Ohel ("tent"), the workers' theater, which developed from amateur performances into a permanent institution with artistic attainments. A number of the larger collective settlements organized musical companies. Visiting artists from abroad showed a partiality for labor audiences, especially in the agricultural settlements, and concerts by eminent personalities were arranged from time to time.

Recreational interests were served by Hapoel ("the worker"), the sports organization of the Histadrut. It encouraged gymnastics, athletics, water sports, and games among workers by providing instructors and playing facilities. Cultural recreation in the form of musical bands, for example, was also included in the activities of Hapoel.

Perhaps the most effective cultural influence of the Histadrut, and a powerful organizational instrument as well, was its press and publications. A publishing house issued original Hebrew books and translations of foreign works. Most notable was *Davar*, a daily newspaper founded in 1925. In addition to news coverage, it provided good literary reading matter as well as expositions of popular science and current economic and social problems. Special supplements were issued for children and women, and a daily page in simple language was provided for new immigrants. Its journalistic standards and general appeal increased circulation until it became the leading daily newspaper in Palestine.

Democracy as a Means and End. The tone and temper within the Palestine Jewish community was democratic, and the ultimate aims of the Jewish National Home as well as the means for their attainment were colored by democratic ideals and grounded in democratic processes. Freedom to differ and to express varying views, equality, not only as an abstract ideal but as a working principle in human relationships, concern with individual differences, respect for human personality, voluntarism in religious belief and practice and in associational loyalties—these and other qualities of democracy were cherished in the Jewish National Home, except perhaps among the ultra-orthodox elements who would have imposed restraints if they had been in a position to do so.

Voluntarism prevailed not only in political and social relationships but also in economic affairs and in the co-operative and collective communities, where doctrine agitated men's minds. Doctrine often breeds intolerance, and the labor movement was permeated with anti-capitalistic ideas; it set its heart and mind upon a new and a cooperative form of society. The economy of Jewish Palestine, however, was basically capitalistic, and even the cooperative and collective movements found it possible to co-exist with agricultural and industrial forms which encouraged private initiative.

The collectives themselves were remarkably free of compulsion: one joined a group freely and one left, if collective living proved onerous or unattractive. And as was noted above, the collectives themselves modified their practices in order to allow for individual differences. In short, social experimentation allowed for freedom as well as equality.

It must not be assumed that the Jewish National Home was a Utopia. There were class divisions and class distinctions resting on economic status and social origin. The masses of Oriental Jews, for example, occupied a lower economic and social position than the Europeans. There was economic strife, with strikes and lockouts, and there were sharp clashes among the political parties and factions.

However, the character of the Jewish National Home tended to narrow the range of difference in status. The idealization of labor cast an aura of distinction about the worker. The cooperative and collective movements encouraged social mobility among agricultural and urban laborers, and increased their earning power. The distinctions between skilled and unskilled workers, and between mental and physical occupations were less marked: all were embraced in the same labor organization. Even the Oriental Jews were not relegated to permanent inferiority. The Histadrut, for example, and its institutions were open to them: between 1939 and 1947, the percentage of Oriental Jews, including Sephardim, in the membership of the Histadrut rose from 7.2% to 12.3%.

The democratic character of the Jewish National Home is attested by the fact that diverse elements were able to cooperate in its development. The devout and the agnostic, the socialist and the capitalist, the well-to-do and the poor were represented in the agencies of the National Home. Except for a fraction of the ultra-orthodox, religious differences did not constitute an unbridgeable gulf. Class distinctions did not result in uncompromising estrangement. Even the doctrine of the class struggle yielded to democratic influences, and the majority of Jewish labor and its leaders were able to work together with bourgeois elements for the attainment of the Jewish National Home.

Development of the Jewish Community. The growth of the Jewish National Home brought into Palestine segments of population differing in language, religious observance, social doctrine, and political orientation. In large measure the ideological baggage brought by the immigrants into Palestine served as the basis for party and group differentiation, but this did not result in insulated fragmentation. The overwhelming majority felt a sense of community which transcended party and factional loyalties, and responded readily to efforts at overall representative unity.

The sense of community had its origins in the common purpose of building the Jewish National Home and in the ideals of national regeneration. It was enhanced by the zealous efforts to make Hebrew the national language of Jewish Palestine and by pride in the solid achievements in social and cultural endeavors as well as in economic and political enterprises. Above all, the feeling of insecurity which the hostile Arab majority engendered, and the conviction held by many Jews that the British authorities were indifferent toward the National Home and not sufficiently concerned about the safety of the Jews, tended to weld the latter into a unit for self-help and self-defense.

The planning and guiding agencies (described above) were a powerful influence in unifying the Palestine Jewish community. The urge to participate in local governing bodies and to influence decisions of broader scope likewise predisposed Palestine Jewry to fashion political organs to represent their views. Finally, the British authorities encouraged limited local self-government and authorized country-wide autonomy in religious-cultural affairs.

In 1921, an ordinance made provision for local councils in rural areas, and the larger Jewish agricultural settlements were thus enabled to elect councils and manage their affairs under close government supervision. This also authorized neighboring settlements to cooperate in joint enterprises like road building. In 1934, a Municipal Corporations Ordinance empowered towns and cities to elect councils for local government. Local rates could be levied and loans contracted only with the approval of the British government authorities. In general, local self-government was closely supervised and restricted.

The Jews took the initiative in fashioning a country-wide representative agency. In 1917, soon after the arrival of the British forces, steps were taken to convene a constituent assembly. Under military administration this was not possible, and a Provisional Committee spoke for Palestine Jewry. In April, 1920, however, elections were held for an Elected Assembly (Asefat Hanivharim) which chose a National Council (Vaad Leumi), and these agencies pressed for recognition as the organs of the Palestine Jewish community. Recognition was withheld for seven years, partly because of the refusal of the ultra-orthodox element to participate and partly because of differences with the government. However, a Religious Communities Organization Ordinance was enacted in 1926, and under its provisions, the Jewish community organization received official recognition during the following year.

Under the Ordinance, the Jews were presumed to be a religious community. But the communal organization sanctioned by the authorities embraced secular functions as well and provided the framework of a semi-autonomous government.

Membership in the Jewish community (Knesset Israel) was not compulsory: while all Jews were listed as members, anyone had the right to withdraw from its jurisdiction. However, only the extreme orthodox group, which counted less than 5% of the Jewish population, actually stood aloof. A Rabbinical Council and rabbinical courts exercised jurisdiction over religious affairs and matters of personal status.

The supreme organ of the Jewish community was a lay body—the Elected Assembly—chosen by direct and proportional suffrage, including women. The Assembly met once a year, adopted policy resolutions, and chose the National Council as its executive organ. The Assembly also voted the budget for the Rabbinical Council as well as the National Council, but its power to impose rates and fees was restricted to educational and charitable purposes. The National Council represented the Palestine Jewish community before the government authorities and administered some of the Jewish public services. The concern of the National Council was with the internal affairs of the Jewish community, and it served primarily as an organ of public opinion. It lodged complaints with the government against inadequate police protection and against policies it considered discriminatory, such as the allocation of grants-in-aid to education and the social services, employment of Jews in government agencies and the like. It represented the Jewish community before commissions of inquiry and submitted memoranda to the Mandates Commission. It laid down policy for the guidance of its constituency on issues affecting the National Home. And it influenced decisions on immigration and settlement, although these functions were considered the exclusive domain of the Jewish Agency.

During the 1930's the importance of the National Council was enhanced by the assumption of administrative functions in education, culture, health and welfare. In the early years of the British administration, the Zionist

Organization and subsequently the Jewish Agency concerned themselves with education. In 1933, however, the entire administration of local education was turned over to the National Council. Its Board of Education enjoyed government recognition, and it supervised the schools under its control and raised the necessary funds, as was indicated above. It also coordinated through its Health Section the various institutions that functioned in the field of public health.

A concluding word needs to be said about the share of the financial burden assumed by Palestine Jewry in the building of the National Home. The psychology was not that of a dependent community looking to philanthropy from abroad to supply its needs. As the population grew in numbers and strength, it undertook increasing responsibilities. For example, contributions to the Keren Hayesod from Palestine amounted to about one-quarter of 1% of total contribution in 1921-1922 (£P 1,000 of £P 388,000); but in 1944-1945, the ratio was £P 164,000 to £P 2,340,000—7%. During 1941-1946, the Yishuv (Palestine Jewry) raised for various Jewish national funds and institutions and for local emergency needs a total of £P 6,379,000. In addition, large sums were provided for education, health and unemployment funds, and religious, cultural, and charitable institutions. The Jews also paid a disproportionate share of government taxes, without receiving an equivalent share in government services. It has been estimated that "the average amount of aggregate payment per capita of the Yishuv was among the highest in the world."

The Arabs and the Building of the Jewish National Home. The far-reaching economic, social and cultural changes entailed in the building of the Jewish National Home were effected in the midst of an Arab majority. It has been noted that the Arab population, or at least its leadership, opposed strenuously the idea and program of the National Home. Apart from political rivalry, however, how did the efforts of the Jews affect the native population? Did Jewish immigration and purchase of land crowd the Arabs out of the rural areas? Were they harmed by the economic measures undertaken to increase the absorption of Jews? Did the building of the National Home result in the neglect of Arab welfare? In a word, was Arab political hostility the reflection of a deterioration in economic and social status?

To set these issues in proper focus, it must be stated first that the building of the National Home was not motivated by the needs of the Arabs. The primary objective of the Jews was to develop Palestine so that it might sustain a larger Jewish community. The question, then, is, Were the Arabs affected adversely by the energetic efforts of the Jews?

In an agricultural country, land is of course of paramount importance. The Jews bought all but an insignificant fraction of the land they acquired: even uncultivated land had to be purchased and reclaimed. The prices paid by the Jews rose to unprecedented heights: in the 1880's, farm land was bought at £I 0.350 to £I 1.100 (in terms of Israeli currency and prices of 1956) per dunam (about one-quarter acre); in 1910, the price per dunam varied from £I 1 to £I 10, according to the quality of the land; in 1921, Arabs of the Valley of Jezreel received £I 15-18 per dunam, and in 1934, as much as £I 50-60 per dunam. Improved plantation-land was sold at £I 70 per dunam in 1910, and at £I 150-200 per dunam in 1935.

The bulk of the Jewish land was purchased from large landowners who were thus enriched. However, small proprietors also profited, and Lewis French, the British Director of Development for Palestine in 1931-1932, reported that sales to Jews had enabled Arabs to improve the cultivation of the land remaining in their possession.

There was much argument over the displacement of Arab cultivators by Jewish purchases of land. The British authorities were properly concerned about this matter, and as early as 1920, took precautions to protect Arab farmers. The Transfer of Land Ordinance of that year stipulated that displaced tenants must be assured of sufficient land in the district or elsewhere. The Jewish purchasing agencies, too, added voluntary gift-payments to displaced tenants, when they felt that justice required it.

The British authorities made the effort to determine the number of landless Arabs displaced by land sales to Jews. They established that by 1936, no more than 664 heads of families had valid claims as "landless," and 347 of these were resettled by the Government. The explanation is simple: a large proportion of the land bought by Jews had been uncultivated and was rendered cultivable through reclamation; and most Arabs who were displaced found no difficulty in securing land elsewhere in the country.

During the years of the Mandate, there was a phenomenal increase in the non-Jewish population of Palestine: the census of 1922 listed 668,258 non-Jews; in 1947, the number was estimated at about 1,319,000. In some measure, this was, of course, the result of British rule—greater security, better health conditions, concern for the welfare of the rural population, etc. But Transjordan was also under British mandatory rule, and Syria and Greater Lebanon were under French mandatory administration, and in none of these countries did the native population grow as rapidly.

The Jews maintained that the building of the National Home was mainly or largely responsible for the conditions which encouraged and sustained the increase in the native population; that Jewish immigration, economic development and social progress increased the capacity of the country to support larger numbers of Arabs as well as Jews. More specifically, they argued that the Jews created effective demand at higher prices for Arab agricultural produce; that Arabs found better opportunities for work and higher wages in industries and services developed by Jews; that the successful drive of the Jews against malaria benefited the Arab population living in the vicinity of the swamps; that the Jews contributed a disproportionate share to government revenues which were used mainly for Arab welfare; that the example of the Jews encouraged Arabs to improve farming methods, develop industry, organize cooperatives, combat usury; in short, that the economic opportunities, improvement in medical and health services, and general social progress which the National Home made possible were in large measure responsible for the improved conditions which were reflected in the growth of the native population. The Jews claimed that the building of the National Home not only resulted in the natural increase of the Arabs but also attracted large numbers of Arab immigrants from neighboring countries.

Many of the Jewish services were available to the Arabs. Hadassah's medical facilities served all who applied, regardless of religious or national affiliation, and some of these facilities were introduced in predominantly Arab neighborhoods and ministered to more Arabs than Jews. The medical services of Jewish agricultural settlements were open to their Arab neighbors. Arabs were welcome in Jewish cooperatives and some not only became members but preferred them to separate Arab societies. Jewish banks and mortgage companies were available to Arabs. Jewish labor organizations made the effort to organize and assist Arab labor.

It was likewise evident that the Arabs shared in the growing prosperity of Palestine. Wages were higher, agricultural productivity greater, and per capita national income larger among the Palestine Arabs than in neighboring lands, including Iraq, Syria, Greater Lebanon, and Egypt. The death rate showed similar relative progress: during the 1920's, the death rate among Palestine Moslems (about 27 or 28 per 1,000) was close to that of Egypt; in the 1930's, it declined considerably in Palestine, but not in Egypt; and by 1941-1944, it had fallen to about 19.4 per 1,000 of Palestine's Moslem population. The average life span in Egypt was 38.50 years during 1936-1938; among the Palestine Moslems, it was 37.5 years in 1926-1927, and rose to 49.5 years by 1942-1944.

The infant mortality rate was especially revealing. Between 1922-1945 infant deaths per 1,000 live births among Palestine Moslems fell from 163.02 to 93.9, but it remained high in neighboring Arab countries. And especially significant is the fact that the decline in infant mortality and the increase in the non-Jewish population were most marked by far in the Haifa and Jaffa districts where Arabs were in close contact with the Jewish population.

The conclusion appears undeniable that the building of the Jewish National Home contributed materially to the advancement of the Palestine Arabs economically, socially, and culturally. The Jews also made some efforts to promote understanding and cooperation with the Arabs. However, all this was not sufficient to allay hostility which became more intense as Jewish efforts showed promise of greater success.

It is true that economic oppression and economic rivalry foment national strife. But the converse does not hold, theories of economic determinism notwithstanding: economic advantage does not necessarily induce national harmony. The Jews and Arabs therefore remained two hostile camps, the one straining to develop the country and make room for homeless Jews, the other determined to stem the tide of immigration and to rule the land as their own.

In fact, Jews and Arabs came to constitute separate and self-contained communities. They lived in separate villages and suburbs and, even in the cities, mainly in separate neighborhoods. The bloody riots and the proclamation by the Arab leadership of a boycott of Jewish business and of land sales to Jews, as well as the campaign of the Jews to buy Jewish products, tended to create a dual economy. True enough, neither the Arab boycott, nor the Jewish campaign for Jewish labor and its products was fully observed: land sales to Jews continued; large numbers of Arabs were employed in Jewish industry and agriculture; and Arab produce was bought by Jews. But the economies of the two peoples were recognizably distinct, partly because of estrangement and partly because the types and quality of products required by Jews and Arabs differed. It has been estimated that sales of Jewish industry to Palestinian Arabs did not exceed 6% to 8% of the general turnover. Thus, independent of the Arab market, the Jewish National Home was virtually unaffected by the Arab boycott in Palestine.

By the end of World War II, the Jewish National Home was a vigorous community, with a dynamic economy, far-reaching social and cultural institutions, and effective political leadership. The Arabs, too, were organized, determined and militant. The British held the reins of government, but weakened by the war and harried by competing pressures, they found it increasingly difficult to impose their will on either Arabs or Jews. A quarter-century of conflict had reached a critical stage, and decisive events were in the making.

— 6 —

FROM NATIONAL HOME TO SOVEREIGN STATE

The Post-War Deadlock. When World War II came to an end in Europe on May 8, 1945, all elements in Palestine were consolidating their positions for the final struggle. The Arab States had joined the anti-Nazi coalition the preceding February, and they had formed the League of Arab States which, along with the Palestine Arabs, opposed any compromise on Jewish immigration.

The mood of the Jews was one of anxious hope, which was nourished by the accession to power of the pro-Zionist British Labour Party and by the widespread sympathy for the remnant which survived Nazi extermination. The Jewish Agency, therefore, focused attention on refugee settlement: it promoted illegal immigration and appealed to public opinion, especially in the United States, to support the admission of refugees to Palestine.

The Jewish cause won powerful support. After receiving a report on the wretched condition of the Jewish displaced persons (*see Reading No. 16*), President Truman requested the British government to admit 100,000 refugees to Palestine (*see Reading No. 17*), and in December of the same year, both houses of Congress resolved in favor of free Jewish immigration and the development of Palestine as a democratic commonwealth. (*See Reading No. 18.*) The British Labour government, however, was not ready to abandon the White Paper of 1939, and countered with a proposal that an Anglo-American Committee of Inquiry study the problem. The Committee, reporting in April, 1946, recommended, among other measures, the admission of 100,000 refugees and the removal of restrictions on land sales to Jews. (*See Reading No. 19.*) But the British government, swayed by Arab threats, failed to act on the recommendations.

These developments exasperated Palestine Jewry. The world had been shocked by the gory record of the Nazi extermination camps, but the surviving remnant of Jews continued to languish in the camps, and no state offered them asylum. Humanitarian appeals had proved fruitless and weighty intercessions unavailing. The Jews felt deeply wronged morally and physically, and the conviction hardened that they must help themselves. The mood became one of desperate courage which inevitably resulted in widespread violence.

Some elements had already despaired of a peaceful solution. The *Irgun Zvai Leumi* (National Military Organization), established in 1937, and an offshoot from that body known as the Fighters For Freedom (Sternists), were in open revolt against the British. The official Jewish leadership, however, pursued a policy of disaffection rather than rebellion, of resistance to the White Paper policy rather than full defiance of the British administration. The Haganah (Defense Units), the military arm of the Jewish Agency, used force to facilitate illegal immigration, but it was under restraining orders to attack the barriers to immigration rather than British personnel as such.

When the recommendations of the Anglo-American Committee of Inquiry were ignored, the Haganah struck at vital communications as a demonstration of force: strategic bridges were blown up and railway workshops damaged. The British retaliated with mass arrests, including leaders of the Jewish Agency and National Council, house searches for arms, and other measures. This only played into the hands of the extremists, and in July the Irgun demolished the Government Offices in the King David Hotel in Jerusalem, causing the loss of nearly 100 British, Arab, and Jewish lives. The Jewish Agency condemned this outrage, but the British did not distinguish between gradations of opposition and took reprisals upon the entire Jewish population. A curfew was imposed upon all Jews, Tel Aviv was isolated for several days, multitudes were interrogated, hundreds detained, and death sentences imposed on terrorists. In August, 1946, the British government began to deport illegal immigrants to

Cyprus—a measure which intensified violence and provoked further repression.

By the beginning of 1947 the British position in Palestine was intolerable and untenable. American public opinion and President Truman pressed for the admission of refugees. The Arabs sullenly opposed any compromise. And bloody repression of Palestine Jewry would not be tolerated by world opinion. Recourse to the United Nations appeared to hold the promise of clearing the air and of breaking out of the baffling dilemma. The British were convinced that the Mandate was unworkable and that their withdrawal would result in chaos, with the Jews at the mercy of the Arabs. Would not the implied threat of withdrawal rally world opinion in support of Britain's policy? The Mandate might then be modified to accord with imperial needs. On February 25, 1947, the British government announced the submission of the Palestine problem to the United Nations.

Palestine Before the United Nations. After extensive discussions, the General Assembly constituted, on May 15, 1947, the United Nations Special Committee on Palestine (UNSCOP) to examine the issues and submit proposals. The Committee unanimously recommended the termination of the Mandate, and a majority of its eleven members proposed the partition of the country into an Arab State, a Jewish State, and a special regime for the city of Jerusalem, with economic union for the entire country. The General Assembly debated at length these and other proposals of the Committee, and on November 29, 1947, it adopted the partition plan (*see Reading No. 20*) by a vote of 33 to 13, with ten abstentions. The United States, the Soviet Union, and France voted for partition. The General Assembly also set up a United Nations Palestine Commission to supervise the execution of its resolution and called on the Security Council to provide for the enforcement of partition.

The Jews accepted partition, but the Palestine Arabs and the Arab states defied the United Nations and prepared to resist. A peaceful resolution of the problem depended on the effectiveness of the Palestine Commission, the forceful authority of the Security Council and, above all, the cooperation of the British government.

The Palestine Commission sought to arrange for a progressive transfer of authority from the British to itself and for the establishment of Arab and Jewish provisional councils which were to function under its supervision. It hoped thus to exercise control over Arab and Jewish military forces, to delimit frontiers, to maintain public services, to protect the Holy Places, and to preserve economic union. The British, however, refused to co-operate because the proposed solution was not acceptable to both parties in the Palestine conflict. They declared that until the Mandate was terminated on May 15, 1948, they would remain in full control; that there would be no gradual transfer of authority; and that the Commission was not to enter Palestine until two weeks prior to the termination of the Mandate. This left Arabs and Jews to their own devices and invited chaos.

The partition resolution required the Mandatory to evacuate a port and its hinterland in the projected Jewish State for the reception of Jewish immigrants. The British government ignored this and continued to intern "illegal" immigrants in Cyprus. Moreover, it imposed an embargo on the shipment of arms to Palestine, but continued to supply arms to Arab states which were preparing to invade Palestine. This undoubtedly encouraged the Arabs to defy the United Nations.

The situation in Palestine deteriorated rapidly: open clashes between Arabs and Jews became widespread early in 1948; Arab bands infiltrated from Syria and Transjordan; and casualties mounted. The United Nations Security Council, however, floundered. For three months, it took no action at all, and by the end of February, 1948, it was evident that the refusal of Britain to co-operate and the increasing turmoil in Palestine had occasioned a retreat from partition. Under United States leadership, the Security Council called upon the General Assembly to reconsider the matter.

The General Assembly met in April, 1948, and debated a United States proposal for a temporary trusteeship for Palestine. But no state other than the United States was willing to participate in armed enforcement of a trusteeship; the Jews rejected it; and the Arabs would not hear of a Jewish state in any form. On May 14, 1948, while the General Assembly was in plenary session, it was announced that the State of Israel had been proclaimed and that the United States had accorded it *de facto* recognition. The Assembly thereupon resolved that a mediator be appointed to seek peace between the Arabs and Israelis.

The War of Independence. Israel's War of Independence began in desultory fighting immediately after the adoption of the partition resolution by the General Assembly on November 29, 1947. The Palestine Arabs, soon joined by irregulars from across the borders, attacked Jewish settlements and vital roads, and clashes occurred in the cities, including Jerusalem. In February, while the British were still in control of the country, open warfare became general, with both antagonists seizing territory, arranging truces, and consolidating their positions.

With the termination of the Mandate on May 15, 1948, the Arab states—Egypt, Transjordan, Iraq, Syria, and Lebanon, with auxiliaries from Saudi Arabia and Yemen —invaded Palestine. They expected an easy victory, but the Jews not only held their positions but made notable gains. Transjordan's Arab Legion, a well-armed force commanded by British officers, isolated the Jewish sector of Jerusalem by cutting the coastal road. But the Jews built a new road—"The Road of Valor"—and relieved the city.

Meanwhile, Count Folke Bernadotte of Sweden, who had been named mediator, attempted to arrange a cease-fire or truce. Israel favored a truce, but the Arab states rejected it. Only when the Security Council warned that sanctions might be considered did the Arab states agree to a four-week truce, which went into effect on June 11, 1948. When the mediator and the Security Council sought to extend the truce, Israel made a favorable reply but the Arab states refused. Fighting was renewed and Israel made further gains. Finally the Security Council ordered a cease-fire, again with the threat of possible sanctions against the recalcitrant party. On July 18, 1948, the second truce went into effect, this time without a time limit.

Outbreaks and clashes continued during 1948-1949, but the efforts of the mediator and warnings of the Security Council kept the situation in hand. Bernadotte was assassinated by Jewish terrorists and was succeeded by Ralph

J. Bunche as acting mediator. In 1949, Bunche skillfully guided negotiations which resulted in armistice agreements between Israel and Egypt, Lebanon, Transjordan, and Syria. Each armistice set demarcation lines and provided for a mixed armistice commission, with a chairman responsible to the Security Council of the United Nations, to deal with infractions. The United Nations was thus involved in the execution of the armistice agreements.

The armistices brought hostilities to an end, but a peace settlement could not be negotiated. The General Assembly had established a United Nations Conciliation Commission to assist Israel and the Arab states in negotiating peace treaties. Repeated efforts were made but they proved fruitless. The Arabs refused to meet the Israelis in face-to-face negotiations. They pressed for action on individual issues, like the Arab refugees, while Israel sought an over-all settlement. The latter insisted on the *de facto* boundaries, but the Arab states, which had previously rejected the partition plan, demanded the cession of the additional areas seized by Israel, and it was not clear that such cessions would be recognized as a final settlement. The question of Jerusalem, too, could not be resolved. The United Nations favored an international regime, and the Arab states, with the exception of Transjordan, accepted it in principle. Israel agreed to international control of the Holy Places but not of the entire part of Jerusalem which it held. Transjordan, which had seized the Old City of Jerusalem, likewise rejected the internationalization of Jerusalem.

The Outcome. The failure of the peace negotiations left the Palestine conflict in an unsettled state, with the armistice agreements defining a *de facto* situation. However, in countenancing these agreements, the United Nations recognized partition as effected by the war. For the Palestine problem was not resolved by the conciliatory efforts of the United Nations. The Jews had accepted the terms of the partition plan of the General Assembly. The Arabs had rejected it and resorted to war, and the war had resulted in the occupation by Israel of additional territory, which it declined to surrender. Egypt emerged from the war in occupation of the Gaza Strip of about 125 square miles, and Transjordan (reconstituted as Jordan) annexed the remainder of Palestine in defiance of protests from the other Arab states. The Jerusalem enclave which was to have been internationalized, was held in part by Israel and in part by Jordan.

The Flight of the Arabs. The flight of a large majority of the Arabs from Israeli territory was a startling and unexpected result of the war. Conclusive evidence is not as yet available to explain this phenomenon of mass hysteria. The Arabs claim that the Israelis drove the refugees from their homes. But it is incontrovertible that the Israelis were taken by surprise when the exodus began, and that in the early stages of the flight they made strenuous efforts to persuade the Arabs to remain. (*See Reading No. 21.*) There is also circumstantial evidence that the Arab leaders ordered or encouraged the evacuation, possibly in order to arouse war passions in neighboring Arab states and to allow greater freedom of action for the military forces. That they expected a quick victory is well known, and victory would, of course, mean the speedy return of the evacuees.

The terror of war was undoubtedly an important factor in the flight of the Arabs. "Civilized" warfare means that, while combatants might be killed, they must not be tortured or mutilated, and that civilians must not suffer outrage, pillage, or murder. But it was especially difficult to wage "civilized" war in Palestine, with its legacy of bitterness and hatred. In the riots of the Mandate period, atrocities were not uncommon: in 1929, for example, over sixty devout and non-political Jews, including women and children, were savagely done to death. Moreover, in the state of anarchy which prevailed during the last weeks of the Mandate, fighting was done not by disciplined armies which might be held in check, but by small bands which could not be controlled. There were raids, reprisals, ambushes, and other guerrilla tactics. Therefore, the distinction between combatants and noncombatants and between military operations and atrocities became blurred.

This situation was aggravated by two shocking acts of terror. On April 9, 1948, an Irgun unit struck at Deir Yassin, a village on the outskirts of Jerusalem, and massacred some 250 Arab men, women, and children. The Arab response was an attack, on April 13th, upon a convoy from Jerusalem to the Hadassah Hospital and

Hebrew University on Mount Scopus, which resulted in the massacre of 77 doctors, nurses, teachers, and students.

News of terror travels fast, and these atrocities no doubt served to quicken the sense of insecurity into panic. The number of Jews in Arab areas was small, and only about 7,000 fled. The Arab exodus was a mass flight of hundreds of thousands. It must be reiterated, however, that the exodus began before the April massacres and that its full explanation must await further evidence.

— 7 —

STATE AND GOVERNMENT

Recognition of the New State. Israel was accorded recognition by the United States on May 15, 1948, immediately after the proclamation of independence, and by the Soviet Union three days later. Other states followed their example—even the United Kingdom fell in line in January, 1949. By May of that year, recognition had been secured from 54 states, and on May 11, 1949, Israel was admitted to the United Nations as "a peace-loving State . . . able and willing to carry out the obligations contained in the Charter."

The Land. The area of Israel is 8,050 square miles, somewhat less than that of Massachusetts. It forms a narrow strip on the southeastern coast of the Mediterranean Sea, 260 miles in length and of varying width: north of Tel Aviv the country is only 12 miles wide, and its greatest width—70 miles—is south of Beersheba. All its approaches by land are guarded by some 590 miles of hostile Arab borders.

Most of Israel's population lives in the coastal plain, which runs along the Mediterranean and extends in varying depth into the interior. Mountains range eastward from Galilee to Sinai, but fertile valleys, notably the Valley of Jezreel, provide land for settlement. The Jordan Valley and the Dead Sea form the eastern frontiers, and the Negev comprises about half of the entire country. The Negev was until recently undeveloped steppe land or desert, but Israel has begun cultivation of the northern section, and the entire region holds the promise of providing oil and minerals for the new state.

The climate in the north and west is mediterranean, with warm summers and mild winters. The Jordan Valley is hot and humid, and the heat of the Negev is rendered tolerable by cool nights. Rainfall is ample in the north and generally also in central Israel. The development of the Negev, however, depends on irrigation, and most of the necessary water will have to be brought from outside the region. The water resources of the country are limited. The Jordan flows for 73 of its 158 miles in Israeli territory. The Yarkon and Kishon rivers are small. Lake Kinneret is a large body of fresh water but it is distant from the dry Negev. And the waters of the Dead Sea, while rich in minerals, are unsuitable for irrigation.

Israel is a small land, sparingly endowed with economic resources. But its people are determined to develop the natural endowments in fullest measure by means of hard work, imaginative planning, and the ingenious devices of modern science and technology.

Israel's Leadership. The ideals of labor, planning, and science have permeated the leaders and active elements of Israel. The chief architect of the new state has been David Ben Gurion. He has been a dominant influence in the molding of the labor movement, led Palestine's Jews during the last decade of the Mandate and during the War of Independence and, as unchallenged leader of the government since independence, has been a determining influence in the fashioning of state policy and institutions.

Born in White Russia in 1886, Ben Gurion arrived in Palestine in 1906, where he worked as an agricultural laborer and shared in trade-union activities, self-defense, and the development of cooperative settlements. He played a prominent role in the founding of the Histadrut and was its general secretary from 1921 to 1933. He

helped organize the Jewish Legion during World War I
and saw service in its ranks. Elected to the chairmanship
of the Executive of the World Zionist Organization and
of the Jewish Agency Executive in Palestine in 1933, he
became the effective leader of the Zionist movement and
of Palestine Jewry.

Ben Gurion is richly endowed with the qualities of
leadership. He has deep insight and extensive knowledge,
has traveled widely and written and lectured extensively.
He has indomitable courage and determination, and un-
flagging vitality. He combines unbounded faith in the
ideals of Zionism with a realism which enables him to
compromise in order to achieve the attainable. Finally,
he believes in democratic processes and the rule of law.

Chaim Weizmann was born in 1874 in White Russia.
He received a traditional Jewish education and, unusual
for those days, a general education which included science. He continued his studies in Germany, and in 1904
he migrated to England and soon established himself at
the University of Manchester, where he taught and pursued research in chemistry. During World War I he
rendered valuable scientific service to the British government.

Weizmann had been active and had attained leadership
in the Zionist movement before he settled in England.
The cause remained dear to him, and he employed his
great charm and persuasiveness to win the support of
British political leaders, especially during World War I
when he became the central figure in the negotiations
which secured the Balfour Declaration. In 1920 he was
elected president of the Zionist Organization, and he
remained the outstanding figure in world Zionism
throughout the period of the Mandate. In recognition of
his devoted services, Weizmann was elected the first president of independent Israel.

Itzhak Ben-Zvi was born in 1884 in the Ukraine (Russia), where he was active as a youth in Jewish self-
defense during the pogroms and in the Labor Zionist
movement. He settled in Palestine in 1907 and played a
leading role in the building of the Jewish National Home
as pioneer in self-defense and in the organization of the
Jewish Legion in which he served, as teacher, leader of
the Histadrut, and in the organization of the Jewish com-

munity. He was a member of the Jerusalem City Council and for more than a decade head of the Jewish National Council. Throughout these hectic years, he found time for quiet study, research, and writing in Jewish folklore and especially in the history of the Oriental Jewish communities. Even after he was elected president of Israel in 1952, he continued to attend weekly lectures on the Talmud. Dignified in bearing and simple and forthright in manner, he enjoys the respect and affection of his people.

Moshe Sharett was born in Russia in 1894 and was brought to Palestine in 1905. During World War I, he served as lieutenant in the Turkish army and, after completing his education in London in the postwar years, he became a leading figure in the Histadrut and Mapai. In 1933 he was designated head of the Jewish Agency Political Department and soon won recognition as a skillful negotiator and diplomat. He was Israel's first foreign minister and formulator of its foreign policy. When Ben Gurion withdrew for a time from public life, he succeeded as prime minister.

The Provisional Administration. The government of Israel evolved from the Jewish autonomous agencies of the Mandate period—the Elected Assembly, the National Council (Vaad Leumi) and the Palestine Executive of the Jewish Agency. (See above, pp. 34, 74.) In November, 1947, a Joint Emergency Committee was constituted, and this body sought to fill the vacuum created by the disintegration of the British administration. It began the mobilization of persons of military age and took measures to conserve food and fuel and to provide hospital facilities, police, communications, and the like. In March, 1948, a more representative body emerged with the reorganization of the National Council: the latter, reconstituted as the Council of the People, conducted Jewish affairs until the end of the Mandate.

With independence, the temporary administration became the Provisional Government. Chaim Weizmann was elected president, and David Ben Gurion prime minister. The Provisional Government directed the war, levied taxes, set up administrative agencies and conducted essential public services. Jewish immigration received special attention: the very first ordinance of the new state an-

nulled the restrictions of the British White Paper of 1939.
And on the first day of independence, when Jerusalem
was under siege and Israel's fragments of territory were
desperately fending off attacks, when invading armies
were threatening annihilation, and when food and fuel
were in short supply, a boatload of some 500 refugees
from the displaced persons camps reached Tel Aviv. The
Provisional Government took a census of the population
on November 8, 1948. A special committee approved a
draft constitution for submission to the projected constituent assembly. National elections were held on January
25, 1949, and the Constituent Assembly—the Knesset—
met on February 14, 1949, and inaugurated a permanent
government, with Weizmann as president and Ben Gurion
as prime minister.

   **The Permanent Government: A Democratic Re-
public.** Israel is a democratic parliamentary republic.
There is no formal written constitution or bill of rights.
A draft constitution was debated at length in the Knesset,
but it was decided not to constrict the government by a
rigid document during the formative fluid period, but
rather to allow constitutional law to evolve gradually. Individual constitutional laws have been enacted as in England and France, and these laws are subject to change
by the normal process of legislation.

   Human rights, however, are safeguarded. The Proclamation of Independence declares that the State of Israel
". . . will be based on the principles of liberty, justice
and peace as conceived by the Prophets of Israel; will uphold the full social and political equality of all its citizens,
without distinction of religion, race or sex; will guarantee
freedom of religion, conscience, education and culture.
. . ." The program of the first cabinet, approved by the
Knesset in March, 1949, includes as fundamental principles equality of rights and duties for all, including
women, freedom of expression, of religious observance, of
education and culture, and labor rights in significant detail. The safeguards of the Mandatory regime have likewise remained in force, and new legislation has decreed
full equality for women and the abolition of corporal punishment and of the death penalty for murder. In practice,
Israel has maintained the principles of democracy, the
rule of law, and the fundamental freedoms. Representa-

tive government, based on majority rule, has prevailed, and popular elections have been held periodically and peacefully. Above all, the rights to differ and to express varying views in speech, assembly, and publication have been observed.

The President. The president is titular head of the state whose functions are ceremonial and formal. He convenes the Knesset, calls on the outstanding party leader to form a cabinet and receives its resignation when it no longer commands the confidence of the Knesset. He signs all bills passed by the latter, but has no veto power. He receives foreign diplomatic representatives, and names Israel's diplomatic and consular agents after approval by the appropriate cabinet ministers. His discretionary powers include the right to pardon offenders and the authority to consult with various party leaders before designating one to attempt to form a cabinet. The president is elected by majority vote of the Knesset for a term of five years. The first president, Chaim Weizmann, died in office in November, 1952, and his successor, Itzhak Ben-Zvi was chosen on December 8, 1952, and re-elected on October 30, 1957.

The Knesset. The Knesset, the supreme agency of government, is a one-chamber parliament of 120 members, elected for a term of four years by direct, equal, and secret ballot and proportional representation. As a legislative body, it has functioned after the manner of the British House of Commons, and its enactments are subject neither to the scrutiny of a second chamber nor to the limitations of a formal constitution, judicial review, or executive veto.

Moreover, the Knesset exercises extensive controls over the executive. To remain in office, the cabinet must command the support of a majority of the Knesset. The latter ratifies treaties and supervises the work of the executive departments through interpolations and investigations. Control of the budget reinforces the power of the Knesset over the government and administration, and a state comptroller, responsible to the Knesset, audits accounts and reports to the finance committee of the Knesset on the legality, economy, and efficiency of the financial and economic bodies under its supervision. Israel's parliament is quite informal in dress and appearance, but it has conducted affairs with proper decorum and in an efficient and effective manner.

The Cabinet and Executive Departments. The cabinet is governed by the principles of responsibility and unity. Responsibility means accountability to the Knesset: the formation of a cabinet or government is dependent upon Knesset approval, and the loss of support of a majority of that body results in the cabinet's resignation. Unity involves collective support of policies determined by majority vote within the cabinet, and open opposition by a Cabinet member to a government policy is possible only by express permission, which is, however, granted in "matters of conscience." Israeli cabinets rest on the coalition of a number of parties.

The executive departments include the usual ministries of defense, foreign affairs, finance, commerce and industry, communications, agriculture, labor, interior, justice, health, social welfare, education and culture, and posts. There is a separate ministry of police, and special needs account for the ministries of development and of religious affairs. The Prime Minister's Office embraces important administrative units, such as the Civil Service Commission, the Central Bureau of Statistics, the Scientific Research Council, the Atomic Energy Commission, broadcasting and press services, state archives, and others.

Political Parties. Israel is a multiparty state, and all of the Jewish political parties originated or developed during the period of the Mandate. Labor or socialist objectives are represented by several parties. The Israel Labor Party (Mapai) commands the largest labor following and it is the dominant party of the country. Its philosophy is social-democratic, but it seeks to attain the socialist goal primarily through cooperative ownership of the means of production and distribution rather than through their nationalization. Ben Gurion is its outstanding leader, and the Histadrut (in which its adherents are most numerous) the source of its power. Its program embraces political and social democracy and a planned economy which tolerates state-controlled private enterprise. Its foreign policy is oriented toward the Western democracies.

The United Workers Party (Mapam) was founded in 1948 as a coalition of three previously existing left-wing socialist groups. It represents a fusion of Zionism and Marxism and favors a united socialist labor front, including Arab labor, and the rapid socialization of the economy. In foreign policy, it has urged neutralism with a pro-Soviet orientation, but Soviet hostility to Israel has undermined its influence and its representation in the Knesset has progressively declined.

At the extreme left is the Communist Party, a small but vociferous group which echoes faithfully the line dictated by Soviet foreign policy.

Religious interests are represented by three parties. The Agudat Israel is uncompromisingly orthodox and sternly opposed to all national forms which deviate from its conception of traditional ritual and religious lore. The Poale Agudat Israel is a labor offshoot of the parent party, sharing its religious views, but favoring cooperative economic enterprise. Two similar but more moderate religious groups united in 1956 to form the Mizrahi-Hapoel Hamizrahi party. This element seeks to influence Jewish national life in the spirit of religious tradition, but it accepts such forms of modernism as woman suffrage, and it is pro-labor in orientation.

The middle-class vote is divided between two strong parties and several minor factions. The General Zionist Party favors private enterprise, with a minimum of government interference, and aims to put an end to state encouragement of collectivism and party influence in government functions such as education, health, and labor exchanges. Pro-Western in orientation, it desires to attract investment capital and to develop the country without the constraints of class conflict, social doctrines or religious-clerical controls.

The Herut (Freedom) Party evolved from the Zionist Revisionists and the Irgun elements of the Mandate period. Strongly anticollectivist, it stands for "a self-supporting national economy, based on initiative, free competition and increased productivity." Its national aims include the "reunion of the land of Israel," within the historic boundaries on both sides of the Jordan.

Among the minor parties or splinters, the Progressives, a pro-labor offshoot of the General Zionists, have achieved some importance. Factions of Oriental Jews have not proved significant. And several Arab splinters, although neither socialist nor pro-labor, have generally supported Mapai, the strongest element in the government.

Role of Political Parties. Parties play a far more prominent role in Israel than in the United States. They permeate all public life, including trade-union affairs, agricultural settlements, cooperative agencies, even youth movements, housing projects, and athletic clubs. Politics and partisanship are never dormant, and ideological loyalties intensify the atmosphere of zealous rivalry. This is due in part to the fact that the state and its institutions are still in the formative stage and each element is eager to mold them to its purpose. The system of government, too, structured as it is on party affiliation and proportional representation, strengthens the influence of the parties on public affairs.

The Judiciary. This branch comprises religious as well as civil courts. The latter include municipal and magistrates' courts with minor civil and criminal jurisdiction; district courts for major civil and criminal actions and appeals from the lower tribunals; and a supreme court of seven justices, a president and deputy president. The Supreme Court cannot review legislation passed by the Knesset, but it has the power to invalidate administrative actions or interpretations of statutes which it regards as contrary to the "rule of law."

The religious courts deal with matters of personal status. Rabbinical courts have exclusive jurisdiction over Jews in marriage and divorce, and may act on alimony, probate, and succession if the parties consent. The ecclesiastical courts of the Christian communities have exclusive authority over marriage, divorce, alimony, and confirmation of wills and may judge other similar matters if the parties agree. The Moslem courts have exclusive jurisdiction in all matters of personal status.

Judges enjoy tenure subject only to good behavior, and the appointments procedure is meant to discourage political influence. Civil judges and those of the Rabbinical courts are named by the President on the recommendation of an appointments committee, consisting of justices of the Supreme Court, government ministers, members of the Knesset, and representatives of the Israel Bar Association. The judges of the Moslem and Christian religious courts are appointed by the Minister of Religious Affairs in consultation with the respective communities.

Local Government. Local government has been promoted and democratized by the removal of property qualifications for voting and the extension of the franchise to women. Mayors and vice-mayors, appointed under the British regime, are now elected by the local representative bodies. Municipal governments and local and regional councils, elected directly by their constituents, provide for the local needs of about 90% of the population, but they operate under the close supervision of the Ministry of the Interior, and no clear division of function has as yet been determined between the local bodies and the central government.

— 8 —

POLITICAL DEVELOPMENT

Elections and Parliaments. The government of Israel has been responsive to public opinion, and the electorate has shown a mature appreciation of orderly democratic processes. This is most significant because the electorate doubled between 1949 and 1955, and masses of the new immigrants had never voted before and could hardly have been expected to rely on the ballot to effect change in governmental policy.

Three national elections have been held since the establishment of Israel. The First Knesset was elected on January 25, 1949, with the participation of nearly 87% of the eligible voters. Conflicts rooted in religious issues weakened the government majority and occasioned a general election on July 30, 1951. The Second Knesset was then chosen by over 75% of the electorate, and it served its full term of four years. The Third Knesset was elected on July 26, 1955, when close to 83% of the voters cast their ballots.

Every national election has been attended by the clamor of numerous parties and factions, and the fragmentation of the electorate (*see Reading No. 23*) has troubled the press and political leaders of Israel. Close study will reveal that splinter groups have tended to disintegrate, especially since 1951 when representation in the Knesset was denied to any group which polled less than 1% of the valid votes cast. But the Third Knesset still included three labor parties, two religious blocs, and three Arab splinter parties with little, if any, ideological differences.

The election of 1951 indicated a trend toward the moderate parties, with Mapai and the General Zionists gaining in strength and Mapam and Herut declining. In 1955, however, Herut nearly doubled its proportionate vote, while the General Zionists lost heavily and even Mapai suffered a loss in parliamentary strength. However, the latter emerged from every election the dominant party in the Knesset, with one-third or more of the seats.

Cabinet Stability. The governments or cabinets of Israel have been coalitions of parties represented in the Knesset. That such coalitions are notoriously unstable is well known: in France, for example, repeated cabinet crises have undermined democratic efficiency. The cabinet system of Israel, however, has proved astonishingly stable. During its first decade, Israel has had only two prime ministers. There have been eight or nine major cabinet changes (*see Reading No. 24*), but only once (in 1951) did a government fall because of an adverse vote in the Knesset. The remaining cabinet changes have been mainly formal: they followed the election of a new Knesset, the choice of a president, the retirement of Ben Gurion, and his return to public life.

In ten years, three significant shifts in cabinet coalitions have taken place. In 1949, after the election of the First Knesset, Ben Gurion formed a government of the secularist Mapai and the clerically oriented Religious Front, with representation also of the Progressives and the Sephardim (an Oriental group). This was an uneasy coalition, with tensions and passing crises, but it was repeatedly reconstituted, and the alliance of Mapai and the religious parties held together close to four years. The election of 1951 foreshadowed a radical change, because the General Zionists emerged as the second largest party in the Knesset. Both Mapai and the General Zionists were moderate parties, but with conflicting labor and middle-class philosophies. After protracted negotiations, they were brought together in December, 1952, on a practical program of economic development to absorb the new immigrants. The coalition endured until June, 1955, despite secondary crises. It was during this period that Ben Gurion withdrew from public life and was succeeded as prime minister by Moshe Sharett.

The third major change in the government coalition followed the election of 1955, which resulted in the defeat of the General Zionists. Ben Gurion, who had returned from retirement, formed a coalition in November, 1955, of all the important labor parties (including Mapam), the Mizrahi-Hapoel Hamizrahi, and the Progressives. This combination was still in power in the summer of 1958.

The relative stability of Israeli cabinets has been due to a number of factors, of which the most important are the preponderant strength of Mapai and the great personal influence of Ben Gurion, who has served as a stabilizing force. The former, with one-third or more mandates in every Knesset, has been the anchor of every cabinet. The rigorous discipline of Israeli parties has curbed irresponsible action of individual deputies, which has been a serious cause of confusion in France. Finally, continuity of policy has been enhanced by the usual carry-over of most ministers into reorganized cabinets.

Major Public Issues. The issues which have agitated the public and parliament have been concerned with the development of government institutions and with the problems of mass immigration, security, national unity, and economic independence which will be discussed subsequently. Provision was made for Israeli nationality and for coinage, passports, and similar necessities of statehood. The system of taxation and the customs were reorganized. Modifications were introduced in the law and in legal procedure. And, since no formal constitution was adopted, a series of constitutional laws, known as the "small" or "minor" constitution, fashioned the structure of government.

The organization of the National Defense Army occasioned considerable strife. In May, 1948, the Provisional Government prohibited the maintenance of armed forces independent of the government. The members of the Irgun were absorbed in the army, but it made independent efforts to import arms and it sought to preserve its own command. These efforts were suppressed and the Irgun was outlawed. There was also considerable feeling about the Palmach, the tough and spirited striking force which bore the brunt of the fighting in the War of Independence. Some wanted to maintain it as an ideological elite in the army, but in the end this was abandoned. A national army emerged, based on universal conscription of able-bodied men and women, with formal discipline, ranks, and differential rates of pay.

Educational Reforms. During the period of the Mandate, there was no compulsory education in Palestine, and the Jews maintained and supported numerous schools which varied widely in curriculum and orientation. The religious schools of the extreme orthodox were entirely independent, and even the nationally motivated schools were divided into three types, known as "trends." These were differentiated by religious emphasis, secular outlook, and labor ideals, in accord with the heterogenous character of the Jewish population.

With the rise of Israel, steps were quickly taken to fashion a national system of education. In September, 1949, compulsory and free education was introduced for all children five to fourteen years of age and for those aged fourteen to eighteen who did not complete the elementary curriculum. The "trends," however, could not be eliminated at once, and parents were permitted to select the type of school which their children were to attend. In August, 1953, the State Education Law boldly struck at the "trends." The Ministry of Education was empowered to determine standards and to supervise the national schools, and partisan training and selection of teachers as well as administrative control were legally ended. However, the standard curriculum of the national schools has allowed for differences in subject matter up to 25% of school time. Private schools, too, may and do function, but they must meet basic standards set by the Ministry of Education.

Religion and the State. Historical precedent and the character of the population have imposed religious functions upon the state. All preceding regimes, including that of the British, were concerned with religious affairs, and Israel, too, has made provision for the religious needs of its citizens, especially the masses of devout Jewish immigrants from Oriental countries, and for the Moslem, Christian, and Druse minorities. Religion is supervised by the Ministry of Religious Affairs. Religious courts administer religious law in matters of personal status, as has been noted. Religious councils deal locally with public services of a religious nature and enjoy state financial support. Only kasher food is served in army messes and in related state institutions, and orthodox Jewish women may be exempted from military conscription on religious grounds.

The American ideal of separation of church and state does not obtain in Israel, and its arbitrary imposition on the population would entail serious disabilities for the orthodox elements. However, freedom of conscience prevails, and freedom of religious observance and non-observance. Those who desire a religious way of life are assisted, but non-believers are not under control of orthodox practice, except in marriage and divorce, which can be performed only by the orthodox functionaries. There are no religious tests of any kind and, in fact, a large part of the population, including many of the leading officials, are non-observant in the orthodox sense of the word.

Women's Rights. The government of Israel has boldly promoted the emancipation of women, despite the sanction of inferiority by religious and social tradition and despite the vigorous opposition of orthodox elements. The rights to vote and hold office have been extended to women. The Equality of Women's Rights Law (1951) has empowered them to own and dispose of property, even after marriage. They have equal rights in the guardianship of minor children. The qualifications for Israeli nationality apply equally to men and women. Even the laws of marriage and divorce have been modified to woman's advantage: child marriage has been prohibited;

poligamy has been banned; and a woman cannot be divorced against her will, unless sanctioned by a court.

Israel and World Jewry. The Jewish Agency and the World Zionist Organization shared in the building of the Jewish National Home and continue to function under the new state. The rise of Israel, however, made necessary a clarification of their relationship to the state, and in 1952 a law was passed defining their status and functions. The law declares that Israel is "the creation of the entire Jewish people," and that the World Zionist Organization– Jewish Agency are to continue to aid in the settlement and absorption of immigrants. The World Zionist Organization has especially been recognized "as the authorized agency which will continue to operate in the State of Israel for the development and settlement of the country, the absorption of immigrants . . . and the coordination of the activities in Israel of Jewish institutions and organizations active in those fields."

This and other laws have made it clear that non-Israeli Jews cannot wield governmental power in Israel: that is the function of the authorities elected by the people of Israel. Jews of other countries, whether Zionists or non-Zionists, are not citizens of Israel unless they choose to settle in the country. Similarly, the State of Israel cannot exercise political authority over Jews of other lands. A great many of the latter cooperate in the work of immigration and in the development of Israel so that the immigrants might be settled and absorbed. But that, too, is done voluntarily.

However, world Jewry and the Jewish people of Israel have common religious and cultural ideals and institutions. They share the fundamentals of religion, a language, over three millennia of Jewish history, customs, ceremonies, and folkways. But it should be noted that even in this area, the relationship is voluntary. Neither the State of Israel nor its spiritual and cultural leaders possess compulsory authority of any kind over Jews of foreign lands.

— 9 —

POPULATION PROBLEMS

The population of Israel has grown phenomenally during the first decade of independence. On May 14, 1948, the country had an estimated Jewish population of 650,000, and at the end of that year the non-Jewish minorities totaled about 120,000. By the end of 1957 the number of Jews had increased to 1,762,741, that of the non-Jewish minorities to 213,213, and the total population stood at close to two million.

Israel's population consists of three recognizable layers, namely, the Jewish population resident in the country at the end of the Mandate period, the mass of new immigrants, and the non-Jewish minorities. The latter segments have posed formidable problems for the new state.

The "Ingathering of the Exiles." Jewish mass immigration has been one of the basic policies of Israel, and its effects have left their mark upon every aspect of life in the country. The Declaration of Independence announced that "the State of Israel will be open to the immigration of Jews from all countries of their dispersion," and the Law of Return of July 5, 1950, proclaimed *Aliya* (immigration of Jews for settlements in Israel) as a right: "Every Jew has the right to come to this country as a settler." In a memorable sentence, Ben Gurion signalized this principle as the primary purpose of Israel. "It is for this [the Ingathering of the Exiles]," he declared in the Knesset, "that the State was established, and it is by virtue of this alone that it will stand." And the policy has had overwhelming support in parliament, the press, and among the Jewish population.

This passion for immigration may be explained by the vivid memories which the Jews of Israel have of homelessness and persecution and by their deep concern for their brethren who have languished in refugee camps or lived on sufferance among unfriendly majorities. And it has been enhanced by the urge to self-preservation of a small community living among the vast and hostile Arab population of the Middle East. An increase in the Jewish population makes for a greater sense of security. The zeal for immigration has at times expressed itself in the extravagant hope that all Jews will migrate to Israel. But the leaders, at least, understand that the Jewish masses of the United States, and of other countries as well, do not regard themselves as exiles and are entirely at home in their native lands. They recognize that "at all times *Aliyah* has been a product of Jewish anguish," that is, that persecution and insecurity have been compelling factors in Jewish emigration even to Palestine. The emphasis has therefore been upon the immigration of Jews from inhospitable lands where they have suffered discrimination.

The Process of Ingathering. The policy of Israel has been to admit immigrants *en masse* even when the country has not been fully ready to absorb them. The remnants which survived Nazi extermination were quickly transported to Israel, where the victims were received with sympathy and understanding. The camps were emptied of Jews, except for the hard-core cases, and western Europe was relieved of the Jewish refugee problem. The Jews whom the British had interned in Cyprus were likewise brought to Israel, and in February, 1949, the last of the camps were abandoned with festivities in which even the British participated. Large numbers of the surviving Balkan and Polish Jews were destitute and broken in health, but those who were allowed to emigrate found homes in Israel.

The Jewish communities of the Middle Eastern and North African Moslem lands had become reservoirs of refugees even before the Arab-Israeli war made their position precarious. Yemen represented the most backward areas where Jews were subjected to gross and humiliating discrimination and intermittent persecution, including ritual murder charges and mob violence. And life for the Jews was far from secure even in the so-called more advanced countries. Long despised as non-believers, they were adversely affected by the rising native nationalism, and Nazi-Fascist propaganda exposed them to spoliation and worse. Massacres occurred in Libya during 1945, before the Palestine situation became dangerous. A mass refugee problem was developing when Israel came to the rescue.

The Ingathering from Moslem lands assumed the character of mass evacuation. The Jews of Yemen (about 45,000) and of Iraq (about 123,000) were brought to Israel by air lift, popularly known as "Operation Magic Carpet" and "Operation Ali Baba." They were totally beggared, but not hopeless, for Israel wanted and welcomed them. They were returning "home" after a long exile. From these lands and from Libya, the Ingathering removed practically the entire Jewish population, sweeping clean the festering remains of age-old Jewish problems. Israel claimed the Jews who were "unwelcome guests" (a Nazi phrase) in their native lands.

Mass immigration continued until close to the end of 1951, when the staggering costs of transporting destitute multitudes, and of settling and rehabilitating them, compelled a temporary change in policy. The ideal of the Ingathering remained, and small groups who arrived were assisted. But state-financed mass transfers were curtailed, and immigration declined sharply during 1952-1954. By the middle of 1954, however, rising insecurity in North Africa which resulted from the national revolt against French rule induced Israel to resume mass immigration.

The Ingathering in Figures. The results of a decade of immigration (from May, 1948, to the end of 1957) have been startling. Nearly 900,000 Jews have entered Israel, about 685,000 of them during the first three years and eight months of independence. (*See Reading No. 8B.*) And all this has been accomplished by a Jewish population which numbered initially some 650,000. In other words, a heterogeneous population, far larger than the resident community, has had to be cared for and settled while a war was being fought, a state and government fashioned, the borders continuously disturbed even after the formal end of hostilities, and the entire Middle East seething with resentment and shaken by upheaval. To appreciate the magnitude of this achievement, one must recall that a total of some 484,000 Jewish immigrants arrived in Palestine during the entire thirty years of British administration.

Problems of the Ingathering. Overwhelming difficulties have beset the efforts to settle and absorb the masses of immigrants. The economic, social and cultural assimilation of nearly 900,000 persons in less than a decade would have been a formidable undertaking for a small country even under favorable conditions. In Israel, this has been attempted in defiance of obstacles posed by limited resources, an uneasy armistice, regional boycott, and the composition and character of the new immigration.

Unlike the period of the Mandate, when immigration was highly selective and severely restricted by economic absorptive capacity, Israel has admitted whole communities, especially from Moslem countries, without regard to their economic usefulness or the present ability of the country to absorb them. Along with the young and vigorous have come a host of dependents—the children, the aged and infirm, the handicapped and diseased, the mentally and socially maladjusted. And the vast majority of the new arrivals have been totally without means. All have become consumers even before setting foot on Israeli soil, but their participation in production has been a gradual process.

Social and cultural adjustment has been equally difficult. During 1919-1948, close to nine-tenths of the Jewish immigrants had come from Europe or from other "Western" countries. Many of them had received training in the Hebrew language and national ideals, as well as in economic skills, and many had been imbued with social idealism and a passion for labor. But since the rise of Israel, a majority of the immigrants have come from Asia and Africa, and all but a small fraction were without a knowledge of Hebrew and of national ideals and values. Many have been entirely lacking in education or culture in the modern sense of the words, or in appreciation of the values of work and work standards.

Israel has been obliged to undertake the training or retraining of the immigrants for gainful employment. Housing, schooling, and medical facilities have had to be provided, infectious diseases combatted, illiteracy fought, and a heritage of substandard living in slum areas overcome. Indeed, special efforts have been necessary to educate the newcomers in the elementary requirements of hygiene and sanitation.

The immediate needs of the immigrants have been met by planning and improvisation. During the War of Independence and shortly thereafter, the new arrivals remained in reception camps until housing and employment became available. In the summer of 1950, the *maabara* (plural *maabarot*) or transitional settlement was introduced, with temporary housing and employment. Some *maabarot,* set up where employment was temporarily available, were later abandoned. But others were planned for permanent settlement, and the immigrants participated in the development projects which were meant to absorb them. During 1954, still another method—the "ship to farm" system—was inaugurated. Immediately on arrival, immigrants were taken to villages which had been set up with dwellings, schools, and clinics, and they began at once their new life under the guidance of instructors.

All immigrants to new lands suffer hardship, and those of Israel have had their share. But the newcomers have not been left to shift for themselves in a strange environment. The government of Israel has sought to guide the process of absorption, and the entire population has made sacrifices to ease the lot of the newcomers. World Jewry, too, has helped generously with the huge funds necessary to cover the costs. Mass immigration has been a stupendous venture undertaken in defiance of economic realities, but the vast majority of the immigrants have found homes in Israel. The visitor during the past decade has seen not only the dreary reception camps and depressing *maabarot* but also numerous new villages dotting the countryside, with the remains of the temporary settlements still bearing witness to the progress achieved.

The Minority Population. The non-Jewish population of Israel, generally referred to as Arabs, consists of Arabic-speaking Moslems and Christians, with small numbers of Druses situated in Galilee and on Mount Carmel. Estimated at 120,000 at the end of 1948, the minorities increased to 213,213 by the end of 1957, largely as a result of the Family Reunion Scheme which permitted relatives to rejoin their families.

The effort has been made to assure the Arabs constitutional equality and non-discrimination in political, economic, and social opportunities, including the social services. They also enjoy extensive national-cultural rights in matters affecting religion, language, and culture.

Reference has been made to the special religious courts, with jurisdiction over marriage, divorce, the custody of children, wills, and other matters of personal status. Full religious liberty prevails, and the Moslems and Christians are free to observe their respective Sabbaths. The Arabic language has official status. It is the language of instruction in the state-supported Arab schools, and is employed freely in public life. Arab deputies speak their language in the Knesset and its committees, and they hear through earphones translations of Hebrew speeches as they are delivered. In committees, interpreters sit beside Arab members and assist them with the proceedings. The agenda of meetings, proposed legislation, and the main clauses of the budget are provided in advance in Arabic translation. The Official Gazette appears in Arabic as well as Hebrew, and official notices are issued in Arabic for Arab districts. Coins, banknotes, and postage stamps have Arabic inscriptions.

Arab education in the Arabic language has been encouraged and notable progress has been made. Under the Mandate, the British maintained in 1946 some 454 Arab schools for a population of over one million, but only 25% of the Moslem children attended school. (For the Christian Arabs, the proportion was 90%.) In 1957 the Arab state primary schools numbered 115 with 1,064 classes, and these served a population of about 213,000 situated in the 103 Arab villages and the 8 towns which were wholly or partly Arab. The 28,267 pupils who attended elementary and kindergarten classes constituted over 70% of the school-age children of the settled Arab population. (Under the British Mandate, the *over-all* percentage of Arab school-age children in school had been 48%.) The teachers numbered 835, including 243 women, and special efforts were made to improve their qualifications.

The Arabs have participated actively in the political life of Israel. Men and women have voted in parliamentary elections in high percentages: 79.3% of the qualified voters cast their ballots in 1949; 85.5% in 1951;

and 91.2% in 1955. Arabs have sat in every Knesset—three in the First, and eight in each of the subsequent ones. The Arab vote has been divided between independent Arab splinter parties and those which are predominantly Jewish. In the election of 1955, close to one-half of the Arab votes were cast for three Arab parties which have generally supported Mapai, the predominant party of Israel. The latter polled in addition almost 14% of the Arab vote, thus commanding the support of about two-thirds of the Arab electorate. About 15% of the Arabs voted for the Communist Party.

Local government in the Arab areas has been retarded by the lack of experience in self-government, by family feuds, and by the fear that the assumption of local responsibilities would entail taxation. However, local government is functioning in the two all-Arab towns, and some sixteen Arab local councils have been set up. About 40% of the Arab minority have been involved in some measure in local government, but the central government has covered most of the local budgets through loans and grants-in-aid.

In economic and general affairs, the effort has been made to avoid discrimination. The widespread health and welfare services are available to the Arabs and utilized by them. The government has assisted Arab local authorities in maintaining clinics, and it has provided a visiting nursing service and mobile medical units for villages without clinics. Antimalaria measures have been extended to all Arab areas, and Arabs have been trained in nursing and sanitation.

Labor legislation and national insurance apply equally to Arabs and Jews. Equal pay for equal work obtains in government employment and public institutions, in the Jewish agricultural communities which employ non-Jewish labor, and in the Histadrut enterprises. The unskilled Arab laborers in private industry are at a disadvantage, but Jewish efforts to unionize them have resulted in wage increases. And not only are the facilities for vocational training which the government provides available to Arabs, but loans have also been advanced to them by the government to promote the acquisition of skills.

Arabs engaged in the fishing industry have enjoyed government support. Unemployed Arabs have been aided by emergency public works and by labor exchanges. Roads have been built in Arab areas and water works constructed, as at Nazareth, which now has water piped into the homes.

The Arab farmers have been helped by government-supported irrigation works, instruction in modern methods of cultivation, and loans. Considerable difficulty has been encountered by some 35,000 Israeli Arabs whose homes are beyond the borders or unavailable because of security reasons, large-scale development, or other causes. For these cases, legal provision has been made for compensation in land or cash, and the claimants have been able to appeal to the courts when necessary. At the time of writing, about 80% of the Arab agriculturists own their farms, and they have been encouraged to unite in co-operatives to further their interests. Agricultural machinery is being introduced, crops have been diversified, and the yield per acre has increased. Government aid and the ready market for the produce have brought prosperity to the Arab peasants of Israel.

However, some disabilities exist. Israeli nationality is acquired by birth, residence, naturalization, and immigration. The qualification of birth applies equally for all, but residence has been determined by registration and legal entry into the country. This has, no doubt, involved difficulty, but over 90% of Israel's Arabs have acquired Israeli nationality. Immigration favors the Jews, who acquire nationality automatically, whereas Arab immigration is discouraged, and those who are admitted must undergo a process of naturalization.

Security regulations, too, have proved a handicap for the Arabs. Certain Arab areas, especially along the borders, have been under military government, with restrictions on freedom of movement and other confining regulations. The controls have varied with the degree of tension induced by the activities of armed infiltrators, but the tendency has been to relax the restrictions, especially on freedom of movement. At one time, for example, there were 46 closed areas in Galilee, but these have been reduced to strictly border regions which affect about 10% of the Arab population of the region.

In conclusion, one must note the impressive progress made in cooperation and accommodation between Jews and Arabs. The policies of the government have brought the latter economic prosperity, educational progress, improvement in health, and social betterment. Yet there is no doubt that suspicion mars the relations between the two peoples. The Arabs have suffered the shock of military defeat and reduction to minority status. Their time-honored social fabric has disintegrated and even family units have been severed. The refugees on the borders have kept alive the hopes of a return to the old order, and the neighboring Arab states have fanned the flames of irredentism. These factors and old loyalties have predisposed some of the Israeli Arabs to assist armed infiltrators, and fear of reprisals has induced others to cooperate in acts of sabotage. The Jewish majority has taken precautions by imposing security regulations, and these in turn have deepened the estrangement of the Arabs. The progress toward understanding made during the past ten years has been considerable, but permanent harmony must await a solution of the refugee problem and peace with the Arab states.

— 10 —

WELFARE-STATE IDEALS

Until recent years the democratic state of the West adhered to the principle of "free enterprise," which precluded state control of the economy. The maladjustments resulting from industrialization compelled some state intervention in the form of social legislation to help those who were handicapped by poverty and by the insecurities of sickness, old age, and unemployment. Beyond these ameliorative measures, it was assumed that general prosperity and individual security would best be assured by the free functioning of economic "laws." Opposition to "free enterprise" and capitalist economy took the form of socialism, which sought to nationalize the means of production and distribution; or of fascism, which repudiated democracy and employed rigorous state controls for the purposes of national power.

The disruptive effects of two world wars and of unprecedented depression have undermined the economic and social order, especially in the states of western and central Europe, and rendered necessary extensive state intervention. But the Western states have neither abandoned democracy nor espoused doctrinaire socialism. Instead an intermediate form, generally identified as the "welfare state," has been evolving. The latter has preserved the fundamental freedoms and democratic processes, and has combined in its economic structure features of both capitalism and socialism. Its distinguishing characteristic has been the active involvement of the state in economic and social life in order to promote general welfare. As a concept, this means the welfare of the entire community, but in practice the emphasis has been on the well-being of the underprivileged masses. The freedom of economic enterprise of the propertied classes has been curtailed by measures calculated to ensure a maximum of economic and social security for all.

The ideal of the welfare state has long permeated the major efforts in the building of Jewish Palestine. Under the British Mandate, it was confined to the voluntary activities of the Jews, but with the rise of Israel, social security and welfare and cultural progress have become state functions. There is a passion for equality among large sections of Israel's population, and a conviction that full employment and a living wage, health, rest and leisure, education, and culture are human rights. The government has been directly involved in economic affairs through ownership and direction, and it has encouraged cooperative and non-profit enterprises. It has established controls over housing, passed social-security legislation, and promoted health, education, and culture. And state planning has featured the settlement of the immigrants and economic, social, and cultural development.

Land, Labor and Industry. Only about 10% of the land of Israel is in private possession. The rest is held by the state, the Jewish National Fund, and the Custodian of Abandoned Property; and parcels are assigned on long-term lease to groups, institutions, and individuals. Private enterprise in agriculture and industry is permitted and even encouraged, but it is subject to government regulation. Through public corporations, the state directly controls important undertakings, and the Histadrut enterprises comprise at least 20% of the economy.

The wage policy is determined not alone by the productivity of labor but also by the tradition of social idealism and by the force of labor organization. Wages are supplemented by cost-of-living allowances, paid vacations, and social services. Machinery has been set up for the settlement of labor disputes, without curtailment of the right to strike, and collective agreements are encouraged. An inspection service supervises and promotes labor safety and vocational hygiene, and the employment of women is regulated by law.

The National Insurance Law of 1953 has inaugurated the first phase of a comprehensive scheme of compulsory social insurance. Provision has been made for old-age and survivor benefits, maternity grants, and insurance against industrial accidents. All inhabitants, 18 to 67 years of age, are covered, including the salaried, self-employed, and unemployed as well as the wage-earners. Financial stringency has delayed the enactment of health and unemployment insurance, but health needs are met by voluntary insurance schemes, especially the Sick Fund of the Histadrut. The unemployed are aided by planned public works programs.

Housing. The government has concerned itself with the housing of immigrants, has built homes for war veterans and civil servants, and has cooperated in low-cost housing schemes for others. About two-thirds of all housing units built since independence have been sponsored or supported by the government. The Histadrut and some of the political parties have subsidized housing projects for their adherents, and private ownership of housing is permitted but strictly controlled. Tenants are protected against eviction or arbitrary rise in rentals by the state as well as by private owners.

Public Health, Relief, and Rehabilitation. Mass immigration threatened to undermine the high standards of health and life expectancy achieved by Jewish voluntary efforts under the Mandate. Many of the survivors of Nazi brutality were broken in body and spirit, requiring institutional care when transported to Israel. The Oriental immigrants, too, brought with them numerous diseases—typhus, typhoid, diphtheria, filariasis, trachoma, malaria, and others—which were endemic to their native lands. A *laissez faire* policy would have perpetuated mass misery among the newcomers and exposed the resident population to demoralization. But the measures taken by the government and private organizations have been so effective that no major epidemic has occurred.

The Ministry of Public Welfare has furnished material support, medical aid, and rehabilitation services in the immigrant camps and *maabarot,* and it has subsidized over 150 local bureaus to the extent of 20% to 90% of their budgets. The government has also concentrated attention on antimalaria work, sanitation and food hygiene, testing and quarantine to prevent epidemics, the expansion of hospital facilities, and mother and child care.

A large share of the burden has been borne by nongovernment agencies which have functioned nominally under the Ministry of Health. Kupat Holim, the Sick Fund of the Histadrut, and four smaller sick funds have provided health insurance for about 75% of the population, and the facilities of the former have been expanded to serve about two-thirds of the entire population of the country. With a budget twice that of the Ministry of Health, Kupat Holim has functioned in some 600 localities, maintaining 14 hospitals, 14 convalescent homes, and over 900 clinics staffed by about 7,800 professional workers, including 1,400 physicians and over 2,200 nurses.

Hadassah, the pioneer in health work since 1918, has remained a permanent influence. It has continued its extensive medical work, especially in the Jerusalem area, and taken the initiative in promoting mental health, occupational therapy, and preventive medicine. It has set up a family health service near Jerusalem which combines medical, health, and social-service facilities. Medical education, too, has absorbed its energies, and the first medical school of Israel is the achievement of the combined efforts of Hadassah and the Hebrew University.

Malben, founded and financed by the American Joint

Distribution Committee, has centered its attention upon the rehabilitation of handicapped immigrants, notably the tubercular. Some 18,000 of the latter have been treated, and many have been completely restored to health. Sheltered workshops have been maintained for the handicapped, and homes for aged and indigent invalids. Other organizations, too, have lent their aid, among them the Women's International Zionist Organization, and the Magen David Adom (the equivalent of the Red Cross), which operates numerous first-aid stations, maintains a blood bank and ambulance service, and campaigns for accident prevention.

The total achievement of the government and private agencies may be indicated by a few illustrative figures. Between 1948 and 1955, the number of hospitals increased from 63 to 100, and of hospital beds from 4,600 to over 12,200; and in a two-year period (1954-1956), 110 new mother-and-child-care stations were added, to reach a total of 485. The bed capacity in general hospitals was 3.1 per 1,000 population in 1955. (It was 5.1 in the United States and 1.2 in Egypt.) In 1956 the proportion of licensed physicians to the population was the highest in the world, and that of dentists one of the highest. The ratio of nurses (3.3 per 1,000 population) was higher than in Norway, Sweden, and the United States.

Israel's vital statistics show the effects of the energetic medical and health measures. In 1955 the birth rate was 27.2 per 1,000 among the Jews and 42.78 among the Arabs. (It was 24.9 in the United States and 44.8 in Egypt.) The crude death rate (5.77 for the Jews and 8.01 for the Arabs) compared favorably with that of the United States (8.2) and was far lower than the ratio of 19.3 of Egypt. Life expectancy at birth for the Jewish population, which rose during 1949-1955 from 65.2 years to 69.4 for males and 72.1 for females, was close to that of the United States. Infant mortality especially has reflected the dangers of mass immigration and the successful countervailing efforts. In 1947, the last year of the British Mandate, the infant mortality rate among Jews was 29.2 per 1,000 live births. Two years later the rate leaped to 51.75, but by 1955 it was down to 32.5 for the entire population, including the Arabs. (It was then 26.6 in the United States, and 128.6 in Egypt.) Thus Israel has mastered the health hazards of indiscriminate immigration from substandard lands and remains today a health oasis in the bleak Middle East.

Education. The progress in education has been equally impressive. The effects of the legislative reforms—free and compulsory elementary education in 1949 and the establishment of a unified national system in 1953—are evident in enrolments. In 1957 the four categories of elementary schools included a total enrolment of 310,455; of these 196,178 were in Hebrew state schools, 71,082 in state-religious schools, 18,536 in independent schools, and 24,659 in state Arab schools. These figures do not include some 90,000 children in preschool kindergartens, continuation classes of adolescents, and Christian missionary schools which are not under government supervision.

Secondary education is not as yet free or compulsory, partly because of lack of funds and partly because parents depend upon the supplementary earnings of adolescents. However, about one-third of the 26,000 pupils in the academic secondary schools receive scholarship grants. The government also provides subsidies for teaching equipment and other purposes. In addition, several thousand students attend high school evening classes, and some 12,000 pupils are in trade and agricultural schools.

The majority of Israeli schools are coeducational. The curriculum requires eight years of intensive work in the elementary branches and four years of secondary education. The course of study includes, in addition to the common branches, physical education, nature study, agricultural and prevocational work, arts and crafts, and English. Arabic is taught in many of the Hebrew elementary and secondary schools.

Higher Education and Research. Learning is held in high esteem in Israel, and both higher education and research have attained enviable levels. The Hebrew University is the central institution, with an enrolment of 4,373 graduate and undergraduate students (1957-1958), an academic staff of 756, and courses of study and research embracing Jewish scholarship, the humanities, the natural and social sciences, medicine, dentistry, pharmacy, law, agriculture, education, and librarianship. The high standards, the renown of members of its faculty, and the high quality of its productive scholarship have won recognition for the Hebrew University as one of the great centers of learning in the world. The campus on Mount Scopus became inaccessible after the War of Independence, but studies were continued in improvised quarters until a new campus was constructed at Giv'at Ram in Jerusalem.

The Israel Institute of Technology (Technion), situated on Mount Carmel, is a superior school of engineering, architecture, aeronautics and applied science. The Weizmann Institute of Science at Rehovot is devoted to advanced research in mathematics and the sciences, and among its staff are men of great renown. The Prime Minister's Office also includes a Research Council and an Atomic Energy Commission. Recently, two other universities have been founded—the Bar Ilan University at Ramat Gan and the Tel Aviv University, which is developing under the guidance of the Hebrew University. And a large number of Talmudical academies pursue religious studies.

Archaeology—the excavation and scientific study of the remote past—is pursued systematically and also enjoys wide popular interest in Israel. The Department of Antiquities of the government directs this work in cooperation with the Hebrew University and the Israel Exploration Society. In 1956-1957, some forty excavations were in progress, and a partial survey was made of the Sinai Peninsula.

Hebrew Culture. Cultural life is remarkably rich and varied for a small country, and the government plays a leading role in its promotion. Adult education is widespread: thousands of meetings with cultural content are organized each year by the Ministry of Education and Culture; hundreds of lectures are given under the auspices of the Hebrew University; and the Histadrut and other agencies bring popular education even to the remotest settlements.

Special attention is devoted to the study of the Hebrew language, whose development is guided on all levels by a Hebrew Language Academy maintained by the Ministry of Education and Culture. The revival of Hebrew was one of the crowning achievements of the Zionist movement and the Jewish National Home (see above pp. 49-51). When the Mandate came to an end in 1948, over

75% of all Jews above two years of age spoke the language, and over 93% of the Jewish children aged two to fourteen employed it as their vernacular. Its primacy as the national tongue, however, was threatened by the new immigrants, few of whom had command of Hebrew. By the end of 1950, less than 60% of the Jews over two years of age spoke Hebrew, and even among the children the proportion had fallen to about 80%. However, the strenuous efforts of the central and local governments as well as of private organizations have proved effective in imparting a knowledge of the language to increasing numbers of the newcomers.

Libraries are widespread and popular. The most important is the magnificent collection of the National and University Library, and local libraries and reading rooms are maintained everywhere, even in isolated villages and immigrant settlements. Archives, too, of varying types and specialization, are well organized and regulated by law. Books are read avidly. About 1,000 titles appear every year, three-quarters of them original works of fiction, poetry, and scholarship. A twenty-volume Hebrew Encyclopedia is in process of publication and has over 40,000 subscribers.

As many as 23 daily newspapers appear in Israel, 15 of them in Hebrew and the remainder in a half-dozen foreign languages. Some 290 periodicals, including 50 government publications, devote themselves to literature, art, economics, law, youth, etc.

The arts have a wide following, and music and the theater especially have attained high artistic levels. The concerts of the Israel Philharmonic Society are attended by some 19,000 subscribers, and its special performances attract additional numbers. There are other orchestras and conservatories, choirs, devotees of chamber music, and folk and ballet groups. The government encourages these activities and promotes the study of music in the schools.

The theater is represented by four cooperative repertory companies—among them the well-known Habimah and the workers' theater, Ohel—which gave some 2,500 performances in 1955-1956 before audiences totaling over a million. Amateur theatricals likewise flourish, especially in the cooperative villages, the army, and the schools. A special group arranges performances in the immigrant camps and settlements.

Painters of note have settled in Israel, and their works have been exhibited at home and abroad. Arts and crafts are taught in several schools, notably the Bezalel Art School of Jerusalem, and the government and private organizations have encouraged the preservation of the art skills of the new immigrants.

Sports are popular in Israel. The major political groupings maintain sports affiliates, but coordination is achieved through the Israel Amateur Sports Federation which cooperates with the Ministry of Education and Culture in encouraging training and competitive events and in planning the sports curriculum of the schools.

The Cooperative Movement. From what has been said it is clear that the active involvement of the Israeli government in economic, social, and cultural affairs has not stifled individual or group initiative. The cooperative movement is an illustration of the range and influence of voluntarism and the spirit of self-help which is deeply rooted among the Jewish pioneers of the country. The government promotes the ideal of the welfare state, but the latter is frequently embodied in cooperative institutions.

The growth of collective and cooperative agricultural settlements and of their urban counterparts prior to the establishment of Israel has been noted above (pp. 62 ff.). These efforts have continued and been extended, so that by the end of 1956, there were 2,508 active cooperatives with a combined membership of some 750,000. About 78% were working-class societies, and three-quarters of these were affiliated with the Histadrut. But the cooperative movement is not limited to working-class elements: more than 20% of the groups were in 1956 middle-class and other non-labor undertakings. Fully one-fifth of the entire economy of the country is organized cooperatively, and in some fields, like the export of citrus fruit and bus transport, the proportion under cooperative control is as high as 90% or more.

The agricultural collectives and cooperatives were a distinctive feature of the Jewish National Home, and their numbers have grown under the state. (*See Reading*

No. 25.) But the cooperative movement embraces also marketing and processing agencies, societies for irrigation, insurance, housing, credit and mutual assistance, savings, industrial production, various services, and transportation.

However, new conditions have had important effects upon the cooperative movement. Through the Ministry of Labor, the government now supervises the work of the cooperatives, settles disputes among them, promotes education in administrative techniques and performs the work of research and statistical tabulation. The ideals of cooperative living have also undergone change as a result of mass immigration and the shortage of trained manpower. Some of the *kibbutzim* have been obliged to employ hired labor, mainly in construction and in industrial enterprises. The new arrivals, lacking in understanding of cooperative ideals and methods, have often demanded immediate payment for work done, and their wishes have been met by various improvisations. For example, a special company, established by the older agricultural settlements, has supervised the work of immigrant settlers and paid them in wages and a share of the profits. In the initial stages, the company has borne the losses, but gradually the immigrants have been taught to share in the losses as well as the profits.

Conclusion. The welfare state is often confused with the regimentation of totalitarian regimes. So far as Israel is concerned, no such parallel can be drawn. The essence of totalitarianism is compulsion, regimentation, and the denial of the right to differ, none of which apply to Israel. There, differences are freely expressed, voluntarism permeates the entire pattern of life, and democratic processes function effectively. The state supervises voluntary associations, but it neither destroys them nor uses them as instruments of power.

— 11 —

ECONOMIC REALITIES

The policy of mass immigration and the pursuit of welfare ideals have elicited considerable criticism because both have been undertaken in defiance of economic realities. The known natural resources of Israel have been relatively meager. Agricultural expansion has depended upon irrigation which is costly, and the development of the moderate water resources has been hampered by the hostility of the neighboring Arab states. Deficiencies in industrial raw materials and in power resources have likewise thwarted large-scale industrial development. Clearly the economy of Israel would hardly warrant mass immigration or advanced welfare policies.

However, nations and cultures are not fashioned solely by economic forces. Ideals often serve as powerful influences, and the urgency of need, especially when motivated by ideals, can stimulate effort and ingenuity to create the economic underpinning for civilized living. The entire Zionist adventure has been so motivated. If neat economic principles had been followed, the early settlements would not have endured and the Jewish National Home would not have been built. It was Jewish homelessness and persecution, the urge to national revival, and social idealism which brought Jews to Palestine and sustained them during periods of trial and discouragement.

The policies of Israel, too, have been motivated by these forces and by the requirements of national security. Mass immigration is the response to the challenge of insecurity at home and in the lands of emigration, and social idealism, reinforced by a powerful labor movement, has prompted the emphasis upon social welfare. The exigencies of economics have served as a brake in the pursuit of national purposes, but the ideals have remained, and the national economy has been employed as an instrument for their realization. In evaluating Israel's economic development, it must be noted that the wage scale has not been determined solely by labor productivity, and that agricultural or industrial progress has not been measured exclusively by its profitability.

Policies. The decade since independence has witnessed three major changes in economic policy. Mass immigration and extensive but largely improvised economic activity marked the period from May, 1948, to the end of 1951. During 1952-1954, the New Economic Policy curtailed immigration and achieved greater stability. Since 1955, the problems of the first period have reappeared, but in a less acute form.

Between May, 1948, and the end of 1951 (three years and eight months) about 685,000 Jewish immigrants entered Israel—a mass which exceeded the entire Jewish population at the time independence was proclaimed. These were years of great economic strain, occasioned by war, heavy defense outlays resulting from the failure to achieve a peace settlement, and a rigorous Arab boycott which sealed Israel off from its neighbors. Yet large sums had to be expended on feeding, housing, and settling the immigrants, who were untrained and could not be used with economic efficiency even when employed. The burden proved too much for Israel's economy.

The government resorted to deficit spending, the issue of treasury bills, and the expansion of credit which, together with the mounting demand upon the limited supply of commodities, created a spiral of inflation and a decline in the value of the Israeli pound. Foreign trade, too, showed alarming deficits: during 1949-1951, exports amounted to barely 12% of the value of imports, and the annual trade deficits rose steadily, reaching a total of some $333,000,000 in 1951. The attempts of the government to check inflation by direct administrative measures such as rationing and price controls proved inadequate. Public confidence waned, and a change in policy became imperative.

The New Economic Policy was symbolized by the official devaluation of the Israeli pound in February, 1952, but its ramifications affected the entire economy. Direct controls like rationing were gradually abandoned. The issue of treasury bills was stopped, and the attempt was made to balance the regular state budget. Credit was restricted, and purchasing power curtailed by freezing wages (except when justified by higher productivity) and by a compulsory development loan. These measures helped to reduce imports, and exports were stimulated by special exchange rates. Immigration declined from over 174,000 in 1951 to a total of less than 52,000 for the three-year period 1952-1954. The effects of the New Economic Policy were evident in increased production, a sharp decline in the foreign-trade deficits, greater stability in prices and costs, and public confidence.

The trend to economic stability was again disturbed in 1955 by noneconomic factors. Disturbances in North Africa, which affected Jews adversely, induced the government to resume the policy of mass immigration. The threat of Egypt's arms agreement with the Soviet and its satellites in September, 1955, provoked greater military expenditures. And the Sinai campaign during the fall of 1956 further strained Israel's economy. Foreign-trade deficits rose again, and inflationary pressures increased.

Achievements. The changes in economic policy have involved modifications of means. The end, which is the full and rapid development of the country, has remained a constant, and it has been pursued with zeal and determination. The achievements have been most impressive, not only in quantitative growth but also in dynamic planning. Roads have been built. The fertility of the soil has been increased and desert and swamp reclaimed through bold irrigation projects. Planned surveys have revealed hitherto unknown resources, and scientific studies have found improved methods for their utilization. Special legislation has been enacted to attract foreign capital.

Agricultural self-sufficiency is still a distant hope, but the progress made during the past decade has been remarkable. The cultivated area has more than doubled, the irrigated area more than tripled, and agricultural machinery has multiplied. Agricultural production has nearly tripled, although less than 18% of the labor force has been employed in agriculture, afforestation and fisheries. It has been estimated that Israeli agriculture supplies two-thirds of the country's food needs, and all requirements in milk, eggs, poultry, vegetables, and potatoes.

Progress in reclamation and in the development of water resources holds the promise of further growth. Between 1948 and 1956, water consumption for agricultural purposes increased more than threefold. The draining of 15,000 acres of swampland in the Huleh area was completed in 1957. A 66-inch pipeline went into operation in 1955, carrying water from the Yarkon River (north of Tel Aviv) to the Negev, and other pipelines are under construction. Arab obstruction, however, has delayed the more comprehensive Jordan River development plan.

The obstacles to industrial development have been formidable. The Dead Sea potash works were destroyed by the Arabs, and operations could not be resumed until a new plant had been built and a new road constructed from Beersheba to Sodom. Industrial raw materials, too, have had to be imported, except for some food products, fertilizers, and the cement, glass, and ceramics industries. Notable progress, however, has been made. Factories have been built for the production of steel, pipes, tires and other rubber products, electrical appliances, paper, fertilizers, automobile assembly, radios, and other articles. The annual output in industry, mining, and quarrying tripled between 1948 and 1956. Construction, so vital for a country of immigration, has been vigorously promoted: housing units comprising over 460,000 rooms were built during 1949-1956.

Transportation and communication have kept pace with agricultural and industrial development. The railroad system, disrupted by the war, has been restored, and railway mileage has been increased two and one-half times. Motorized transportation has been extended. Civil aviation has grown. The merchant-marine tonnage increased from about 14,000 in 1948 to 136,000 in 1957. The port of Haifa and the facilities at Tel Aviv–Jaffa have been modernized, and the development of Elath (on the Gulf of Aqaba) as a major port has begun.

The most important single factor in the further economic development of Israel is the planned exploration and utilization of the natural resources, especially of the Negev. Oil, discovered at Heletz in 1955, is already meeting about 5% of the country's needs. Phosphates, copper, ceramic clay, and glass sand have been found in large quantities. Some iron has been discovered in Upper

Galilee, and indications of other minerals have been noted in the Negev. Experimentation with industrial crops, especially cotton, has also yielded notable results.

Problems. Serious economic problems remain, among them the baffling trade gap between imports and exports. Israel has had a foreign trade deficit, that is an excess of imports over exports, throughout the decade since independence. (*See Reading No. 26.*) Close study will reveal significant improvement in the trade balance. During 1949-1956, imports increased by about 44%, but exports multiplied more than two and one-half times. Exports covered only 11.7% of imports in 1949, while in 1956 the ratio was 29.5%. Furthermore, the composition of both imports and exports has undergone change: between 1949 and 1956, the proportion of consumer goods in the total imports fell from about one-third to less than one-sixth, and that of raw materials rose from about one-third to about one-half; and in the same period, the export of industrial products, including diamonds, increased from about 26% to about 52% of total exports. However, despite these improvements, Israel still depends upon external sources to finance the bulk of its imports.

The annual trade deficits have been covered by grants-in-aid and technical assistance from the American government, German reparations payments, Israel government bond sales abroad, private foreign investments, and philanthropy. Foreign-trade deficits and even indebtedness are by no means unusual for new countries undergoing development. And the factor of philanthropy is an asset rather than a liability—an economic asset in the same sense as foreign remittances and the tourist trade support the economies of various countries. However, dependence on foreign aid is risky, and Israel must achieve greater balance in its foreign trade.

Other major economic problems are the insufficiency of natural resources, the occupational structure and utilization of manpower, the need of foreign capital to finance development, and the Arab boycott. Progress has been made in the field of natural resources: the prospects respecting minerals and oil have been noted; and notable success has been achieved in raising cotton and sugar beets to the extent of 30% and 28% of the country's requirements. But much remains to be done. The labor force, too, must be directed to a greater extent to essential production, a task which depends upon intensive training, especially of the immigrants, and on capital for the expansion of productive industries. Foreign capital is a fundamental need for Israel, as for so many other underdeveloped countries; perhaps more so, because the arbitrary reduction of imports or the diversion of funds from public services to investment would reduce living standards and endanger the ideal of the welfare state.

Finally, the economic progress of Israel entails not only the development of the country but also the creation of essential resources and of an effective labor and managerial force. Arable land must be created through irrigation. Minerals must be found and exploited, and industrial raw materials grown and developed. The human material of the immigrants must be trained and welded into a labor force, and managerial skill must be acquired. The cost of production must be reduced to enable Israeli products to compete in world markets. And Israel requires peace and security, so that money and manpower will not be diverted to military purposes.

— 12 —

INTERNATIONAL RELATIONS

As a new and small state, Israel has been obliged to establish diplomatic and commercial relations with the various states of the world, to formalize its status in the United Nations and its agencies, to win acceptance among the Arab states of the Middle East, and to steer cautiously in the treacherous currents of East-West relations. The beginnings were auspicious enough. The United States and the Soviet Union were among the first to accord Israel recognition, and both voted for its admission into the United Nations. France was friendly, relations with Britain improved rapidly, and a large majority of the other states soon entered into proper relations with Israel. However, the hostility of the Arab states has bedeviled Israel international relations and incited the Soviet and its satellites to assume a malevolent attitude to the new state.

Israel's foreign policy, characterized successively as "neutrality," "non-identification," and "independence," has aimed to preserve freedom of action, without automatic commitments or political alignments with the East or West. In accord with this policy, Israel recognized the People's Republic of China, which the Soviet bloc favored, but supported United Nations action against North Korean aggression, which was sponsored by the West. However, the attitude of the powers toward Israel has been determined by global and regional considerations rather than by its policy decisions.

Israel and the United Nations. Israel has participated in the General Assembly and its committees as well as in the specialized agencies, and its representatives at the United Nations have been of superior competence. It has ratified various international conventions, among them the Genocide Convention and the declaration on compulsory jurisdiction of the International Court of Justice. In 1952 an international symposium on desert research was held in Jerusalem under the auspices of UNESCO. And in 1953 Israel was honored by the election of its representative as a vice-president of the General Assembly.

More recently, Israel's eagerness to share actively in the work of the United Nations has waned. The failure of the latter to bring peace to the Middle East, the increased influence of the Arab states exercised through the Arab-Asian bloc, and the impunity with which the Arabs have been able to attack Israel from the United Nations rostrum have discouraged the Israeli government and people.

The Jerusalem issue has likewise embarrassed Israel in the United Nations. The Partition Resolution of November 29, 1947, and another General Assembly resolution in December, 1949, declared for the internationalization of Jerusalem. Israel has favored "functional internationalization," that is an international regime for the

Holy Places but not international government for the entire territory of Jerusalem. The Arab states flouted the Partition Resolution, including the proposed internationalization of Jerusalem, and resorted to war in defiance of the United Nations. Jordan, which has occupied the old city of Jerusalem, has rejected internationalization. But the other Arab states now argue for an international regime, in order, say the Israelis, to embarrass Israel. During the 1950's the General Assembly has considered the question again, but the necessary majority has not been secured either for a limited international control of the Holy Places or for the reaffirmation of internationalization. In principle, therefore, the resolution of December, 1949, remains in force.

Finally, the Arab refugees have compromised Israel's international position. Funds have had to be raised for the support of the mass of uprooted humanity, and the United Nations has repeatedly grappled with the problem. A solution is imperative, and repatriation has appeared to many as the simplest way out. Israel, however, has argued that the flight of the Arabs was the issue of war which the Arab states had precipitated, that Arab leadership had encouraged the exodus, and that repatriation in the climate of Arab hostility would undermine its existence. Proposals have been made for the resettlement of the bulk of the refugees, but the Arab states have declined to cooperate, and they have made effective use both of the issue and of individual refugees in their conflict with Israel.

Hostility of the Arab States. The Arab states have refused to recognize the existence of Israel, and their leaders have openly voiced their determination to see to its destruction. To this end, they have pursued a policy of encirclement, non-communication, economic boycott, and harassment along the borders and in the United Nations.

All of the land borders of Israel have been sealed off, and except for the Mixed Armistice Commissions, no contact with Israel has been permitted. Even foreigners cannot normally enter or leave Israel by way of adjoining Arab states, for the latter have denied visas to travelers holding a visa to Israel. The non-intercourse policy has even affected international conferences and regional agencies of the United Nations. The Arab states were successful in barring Israel from the Asian-African Conference at Bandung in 1955, and they have refused to participate in conferences, seminars, or educational institutes held under United Nations auspices anywhere in the Middle East, if Israel is included. The acquiescence of the international bodies has resulted in the exclusion of Israel from the regional activities of such agencies as the World Health Organization and the Food and Agricultural Organization.

A rigorous boycott of Israel has been enforced. It has hampered water development projects within Israel and has been an important factor in blocking elaborate irrigation plans for the Jordan River Valley, which would have benefited the Arabs as well as Israel. Trade with Israel has not been permitted, and even foreign firms which deal with Israel have been threatened with exclusion from Arab lands. Ships calling at Israeli ports have been blacklisted and denied facilities or services at Arab ports. Goods consigned to Israel have been seized. Commercial aircraft serving Israel have been forbidden to fly over Arab territory. The boycott propaganda has actually reached out to foreign business organizations owned by Jews, regardless of their trade relations or lack of relations with Israel.

Israel argues that the acquiescence of the powers has encouraged the Arabs in their restrictive measures, which menace peace and violate at least the spirit of the United Nations Charter. It is true that when ignored or challenged, Arab threats have not materialized. In 1952, when West Germany and Israel were negotiating a reparations settlement, the former disregarded Arab boycott threats without serious consequences. Similarly, the airlines were warned in 1954 that they would be barred from Arab countries if any of their planes touched Israel, but an effective protest put an end to the threat. The United States Government, however, has yielded to the demand of Saudi Arabia that no Jewish personnel be included among American forces stationed at the Dharan air base —a serious discrimination against American Jews.

The blockade of Israel, extended to the Suez Canal and the Gulf of Aqaba, is clearly in violation of international law. The Constantinople Convention of 1888 stipulates that all ships be allowed free passage through

the Suez Canal even in wartime. But all Israeli ships have
been barred, and goods consigned to Israel on other ships
have been seized. The Security Council of the United
Nations has censured Egypt for "unjustified interference
with the rights of Nations," but the latter has continued
its policy. In 1954 the Security Council again considered
a resolution expressing grave concern over Egypt's failure
to heed its previous decision, but the negative vote of the
Soviet Union precluded any further action. A Soviet veto
also prevented any decision on the blockade of the Gulf
of Aqaba.

Armed clashes along the Israeli borders have perpetuated a state of tension and seriously affected Israel's
foreign relations. The presence of refugees on the frontiers and the enmity of the Arab states have created a
maximum of suspicion and conflict. "Infiltrators" have
penetrated Israel in small bands and perpetrated theft,
sabotage, and murder. Trained and armed commando
units, known as *fedayeen,* have likewise operated from
bases such as Gaza and Sinai, attacking border patrols,
mining roads, wrecking houses, and engaging in other
forms of sabotage which have resulted in loss of life. Fear
and suspicion have occasioned conflicts over violations
of provisions of the Armistice Agreements by both sides.
There have been thousands of charges and counter-
charges, many of which have been investigated by the
Mixed Armistice Commissions. But the latter have been
able to do little more than to make findings in favor of
one or the other of the parties. The outrages have continued.

To discourage *fedayeen* and infiltrator attacks, Israel
has resorted to raids in force as reprisals. The most serious raid occurred in October, 1953, after the murder of
a Jewish woman and her two children. The Jordanian
village of Kibya was attacked and some 53 men, women,
and children were killed. The Security Council severely
censured Israel, despite its plea that the raid was the result
of provocation and border harassment; that hundreds of
Israelis, including women and children, had been killed
by Arab marauders with the connivance and assistance of
the Arab states; that the alternative would be private
vengeance by Jewish irregulars.

Israel was clearly at a disadvantage. Small Arab bands

are difficult to apprehend and they can be disowned as irresponsible irregulars. A raid in force, however, involves the Israeli authorities. The relatively large number of victims resulting from a raid has dramatic appeal, while the murder of a few Israelis at a time is quickly forgotten. Since Kibya, Israeli reprisals have been directed against military posts and bases, but legally the United Nations cannot countenance reprisals of any kind.

The root of the evil has been the lack of a peace settlement and the continuance of a precarious armistice. (*See Reading No. 28 for Israel's "Blueprint for Peace."*) An armistice is a temporary condition between war and peace. When it continues for a long period, conflict is inevitable. And the failure to achieve peace has been due, in part at least, to the divided world, in which East and West have used the Middle East as a pawn in their struggle for power.

The East-West Conflict. The Arab Middle East has great economic and strategic value. Western Europe is dependent upon the oil supplies of the region, and huge investments in oil properties have won the Arabs powerful friends. The Soviet Union has sought to use the Arabs as a means for the penetration of the Middle East, and the Western powers have courted them as an aid in the containment of the Soviet Union.

The United States has been friendly to Israel and generous with economic aid, and it as well as Britain and France have been eager to maintain peace and stability in the Middle East. The three powers, therefore, issued a declaration on May 25, 1950, opposing an arms race in the region and "the use of force or the threat of force between any of the states in that area." (*See Reading No. 27.*) But the desire to contain the Soviet Union has led to the establishment of an American base at the Dharan airport, and to the negotiation of the Baghdad Pact in 1955. Since this policy has sought also to strengthen the military potential of the Arab states, Israel, which has been excluded from the alliance, has felt threatened. It has protested against the arms build-up of its enemies and pleaded for an effective guarantee of its frontiers. But the pleas have remained unanswered.

Soviet policy has been increasingly pro-Arab. During 1952-1953, and especially after the infamous Jewish doctors trial, the Soviet Union became blatantly anti-Israel and even anti-Semitic, and since then, the Arabs have had strong Soviet support against Israel. However, Soviet policy has been determined by the exigencies of power politics rather than by ideological considerations.

The Soviet Union tolerates no outside interference in its sphere of influence in eastern Europe, but it recognizes no such limitations upon itself beyond its imperial domains, and it has especially sought to penetrate the Middle East. The policy toward Israel has been conditioned by the latter objective. Although world communism has always been hostile to Zionism, the Soviet Union and its satellites favored the establishment of Israel, because the termination of the Mandate held the promise of dislodging the British from Palestine. Israel, however, has not served and cannot serve Soviet purposes. Its stand against aggression in Korea and its independent foreign policy have not been in keeping with that of a faithful satellite. Besides, the Arabs are more numerous, they are not beholden to the West, and their sense of grievance can be more easily exploited. The Soviet Union has therefore become the champion of the Arabs.

By 1955, Israel found itself dangerously isolated. The Soviet Union was hostile. The United States and the United Kingdom were committed to the Baghdad Pact from which Israel was excluded. And the United Nations could neither bring peace to the Middle East nor prevent economic warfare against Israel. Border attacks and harassments continued, and Israel felt that these were viewed by the powers in the light of fine legal formulas rather than as the inevitable consequence of the latent state of war which the Arabs perpetuated. A mood of pessimism swept the country, and people and government feared that as a pawn in the maneuvering of the powers, they might be sacrificed in the cause of appeasement. The arms deal between Egypt and Czechoslovakia turned this pessimism into bitterness. Israel felt in mortal peril, for the Arabs were about to secure the means of making good their threats. It determined to act before it was too late.

The Sinai Campaign. During 1955-1956, Soviet arms accumulated in Egypt and a military build-up was effected in the Sinai Desert. In the fall of 1956, Egypt formed a unified military command with Jordan and Syria. Regarding these measures as directed against its security, Israel struck on October 29, 1956, and it quickly cleared the Egyptians out of the Gaza Strip and Sinai, and lifted the blockade of the Gulf of Aqaba. For their own reasons, British and French forces attacked the Suez Canal area. The occupied regions have since been relinquished as a result of United Nations action, induced by United States and Soviet pressure. But the Sinai campaign has had important results for Israel. The Egyptian military preparations in the Sinai Desert have been disrupted. A United Nations Emergency Force has put an end to the blockade of the port of Eilat and to *fedayeen* raids along the Egyptian border. Support by Britain and especially by France has indicated that Israel is no longer isolated. And notice has been served that Israel would not submit passively to armed attack or to partition of the Munich variety.

However, the fundamental problems remain. The Arab states are still hostile and even more impervious to compromise. The efforts to develop the country's economy and to build a welfare state are still thwarted by regional isolation and boycott. Tensions still rack the Middle East, inviting foreign intervention and menacing the peace and security of the region and the entire world.

Part II

READINGS

— Reading No. 1 —

THE BASLE PROGRAM, AUGUST, 1897[1]

The first Zionist Congress met in Basle, Switzerland, on August 29-31, 1897, and formulated the following objectives, which have come to be known as the Basle Program.

✦   ✦   ✦

Zionism strives to create for the Jewish people a home in Palestine secured by public law. The Congress contemplates the following means to the attainment of this end:—

1. The promotion on suitable lines, of the colonization of Palestine by Jewish agricultural and industrial workers.

2. The organization and binding together of the whole of Jewry by means of appropriate institutions, local and international, in accordance with the laws of each country.

3. The strengthening and fostering of Jewish national sentiment and consciousness.

4. Preparatory steps towards obtaining Government consent, where necessary, to the attainment of the aim of Zionism.

[1] *Protokoll des I. Zionistenkongresses in Basel vom 29 bis 31 August 1897* (Prag, 1911), p. 131. See also N. Sokolow, *History of Zionism: 1600-1918* (London, 1919), I, 268-269.

— Reading No. 2 —

THE BALFOUR DECLARATION, NOVEMBER 2, 1917[2]

During World War I, Zionist spokesmen under the leadership of Chaim Weizmann sought to influence the British Government in favor of their aspirations. For its own reasons, the latter decided in 1917 to espouse the cause of a Jewish National Home in Palestine. After consultation with the Zionist leaders, the British Government issued the Balfour Declaration on November 2, 1917. It was addressed to Lord Lionel Walter Rothschild and signed by Arthur James Balfour, the Foreign Minister.

Foreign Office,
November 2nd, 1917

Dear Lord Rothschild,

I have much pleasure in conveying to you, on behalf of His Majesty's Government, the following declaration of sympathy with Jewish Zionist aspirations which has been submitted to, and approved by, the Cabinet:—

"His Majesty's Government view with favour the establishment in Palestine of a national home for the Jewish people, and will use their best endeavours to facilitate the achievement of this object, it being clearly understood that nothing shall be done which may prejudice the civil and religious rights of existing non-Jewish communities in Palestine, or the rights and political status enjoyed by Jews in any other country."

I should be grateful if you would bring this declaration to the knowledge of the Zionist Federation.

Yours sincerely,
ARTHUR JAMES BALFOUR

[2] *Zionism* (Handbook Prepared under the Direction of the Historical Section of the Foreign Office, No. 162, London, 1920), p. 44; Sokolow, cited, II, 83.

— Reading No. 3 —

THE MANDATE FOR PALESTINE, JULY 24, 1922—EXTRACTS[3]

In its general provisions, the Palestine Mandate conformed to the pattern of the "A" Mandates of the Middle East. However, special articles were inserted for the furtherance of the Jewish National Home, and at the request of the United Kingdom, it was decided to exclude Transjordan from the projected Jewish National Home. The Mandate was approved by the Council of the League of Nations on July 24, 1922, and went into effect on September 29, 1923.

✗   ✗   ✗

.   .   .   .

Whereas the Principal Allied Powers have also agreed that the Mandatory should be responsible for putting into effect the declaration originally made on November 2nd, 1917, by the Government of His Britannic Majesty, and adopted by the said Powers, in favour of the establishment in Palestine of a national home for the Jewish people, it being clearly understood that nothing should be done which might prejudice the civil and religious rights of existing non-Jewish communities in Palestine, or the rights and political status enjoyed by Jews in any other country; and

Whereas recognition has thereby been given to the historical connection of the Jewish people with Palestine and to the grounds for reconstituting their national home in that country. . . .

ARTICLE 2. The Mandatory shall be responsible for placing the country under such political, administrative and economic conditions as will secure the establishment of the Jewish national home, as laid down in the preamble, and the development of self-governing institutions,

[3] Great Britain, *Parliamentary Papers*, 1922, Cmd. 1785, pp. 1-11.

and also for safeguarding the civil and religious rights of all the inhabitants of Palestine, irrespective of race and religion.

ARTICLE 3. The Mandatory shall, so far as circumstances permit, encourage local autonomy.

ARTICLE 4. An appropriate Jewish agency shall be recognized as a public body for the purpose of advising and co-operating with the Administration of Palestine in such economic, social and other matters as may affect the establishment of the Jewish National home and the interests of the Jewish population in Palestine, and, subject always to the control of the Administration, to assist and take part in the development of the country. . . .

ARTICLE 6. The Administration of Palestine, while ensuring that the rights and position of other sections of the population are not prejudiced, shall facilitate Jewish immigration under suitable conditions and shall encourage, in co-operation with the Jewish agency referred to in Article 4, close settlement by Jews on the land, including State lands and waste lands not required for public purposes.

ARTICLE 7. The Administration of Palestine shall be responsible for enacting a nationality law. There shall be included in this law provisions framed so as to facilitate the acquisition of Palestinian citizenship by Jews who take up their permanent residence in Palestine. . . .

ARTICLE 15. . . . No discrimination of any kind shall be made between the inhabitants of Palestine on the ground of race, religion or language. No person shall be excluded from Palestine on the sole ground of his religious belief. . . .

ARTICLE 22. English, Arabic and Hebrew shall be the official languages of Palestine. Any statement or inscription in Arabic on stamps or money in Palestine shall be repeated in Hebrew, and any statement or inscription in Hebrew shall be repeated in Arabic.

ARTICLE 25. In the territories lying between the Jordan and the eastern boundary of Palestine as ultimately determined, the Mandatory shall be entitled, with the consent of the Council of the League of Nations, to postpone or withhold application of such provisions of this mandate as he may consider inapplicable to the existing local conditions. . . .

— Reading No. 4 —

THE JOINT CONGRESSIONAL RESOLUTION ON THE JEWISH NATIONAL HOME, JUNE 30, 1922 [4]

The United States Government endorsed the policy of the Jewish National Home. The following resolution was adopted by the Senate on May 3, 1922, and by the House of Representatives on June 30, 1922. It was signed by President Harding on September 21, 1922.

✸   ✸   ✸

Whereas the Jewish people have for many centuries believed in and yearned for the rebuilding of their ancient homeland; and

Whereas owing to the outcome of the World War and their part therein, the Jewish people are to be enabled to recreate and reorganize a national home in the land of their fathers, which will give to the House of Israel its long-denied opportunity to reestablish a fruitful Jewish life and culture in the ancient Jewish land: therefore be it Resolved by the Senate and House of Representatives of the United States of America in Congress assembled, that the United States of America favors the establishment in Palestine of a national home for the Jewish people, it being clearly understood that nothing shall be done which may prejudice the civil and religious rights of Christian and all other non-Jewish communities in Palestine, and that the holy places and religious buildings and sites in Palestine shall be adequately protected.

[4] *U.S., Congressional Record*, 67th Cong., 2nd Session (June 30, 1922), p. 9800.

— Reading No. 5 —

BRITISH STATEMENT OF POLICY ON PALESTINE, MAY 17, 1939 (THE WHITE PAPER OF 1939)— EXTRACTS[5]

The deadlock in Palestine and the fear of Nazi and Italian Fascist propaganda among the Arabs induced the Chamberlain Government to appease the Arabs in order to preserve imperial interests. While rendering lip service to the Jewish National Home, this statement of policy in fact repudiated the basic commitments of the Mandate. The important sections which follow provided for the curtailment of Jewish immigration and land sales to Jews, and projected an independent Palestine state with an Arab majority.

✓   ✓   ✓

I—THE CONSTITUTION

. . . His Majesty's Government make the following declaration of their intentions regarding the future government of Palestine:—

(1) The objective of His Majesty's Government is the establishment within ten years of an independent Palestine State in such treaty relations with the United Kingdom as will provide satisfactorily for the commercial and strategic requirements of both countries in the future. This proposal for the establishment of the independent State would involve consultation with the Council of the League of Nations with a view to the termination of the Mandate.

(2) The independent State should be one in which Arabs and Jews share in government in such a way as

[5] Great Britain, *Parliamentary Papers,* 1939, Cmd. 6019, pp. 1-12.

to ensure that the essential interests of each community are safeguarded.

(3) The establishment of the independent State will be preceded by a transitional period throughout which His Majesty's Government will retain responsibility for the government of the country. During the transitional period the people of Palestine will be given an increasing part in the government of their country. Both sections of the population will have an opportunity to participate in the machinery of government, and the process will be carried on whether or not they both avail themselves of it.

(8) His Majesty's Government will do everything in their power to create conditions which will enable the independent Palestine State to come into being within ten years. If, at the end of ten years, it appears to His Majesty's Government that, contrary to their hope, circumstances require the postponement of the establishment of the independent State, they will consult with representatives of the people of Palestine, the Council of the League of Nations and the neighbouring Arab States before deciding on such a postponement. . . .

II—IMMIGRATION

.   .   .   .

(1) Jewish immigration during the next five years will be at a rate which, if economic absorptive capacity permits, will bring the Jewish population up to approximately one-third of the total population of the country. Taking into account the expected natural increase of the Arab and Jewish populations, and the number of illegal Jewish immigrants now in the country, this would allow of the admission, as from the beginning of April this year, of some 75,000 immigrants over the next five years. These immigrants would, subject to the criterion of economic absorptive capacity, be admitted as follows:—

(a) For each of the next five years a quota of 10,000 Jewish immigrants will be allowed, on the understanding that a shortage in any one year may be added to the quotas for subsequent years, within the five-year period, if economic absorptive capacity permits.

(*b*) In addition, as a contribution towards the solution of the Jewish refugee problem, 25,000 refugees will be admitted as soon as the High Commissioner is satisfied that adequate provision for their maintenance is ensured, special consideration being given to refugee children and dependents. . . .

(3) After the period of five years no further Jewish immigration will be permitted unless the Arabs of Palestine are prepared to acquiesce in it.

(4) His Majesty's Government are determined to check illegal immigration, and further preventive measures are being adopted. The numbers of any Jewish illegal immigrants who, despite these measures, may succeed in coming into the country and cannot be deported will be deducted from the yearly quotas.

15. His Majesty's Government are satisfied that, when the immigration over five years which is now contemplated has taken place, they will not be justified in facilitating, nor will they be under any obligation to facilitate, the further development of the Jewish National Home by immigration regardless of the wishes of the Arab population.

III.—LAND.

16. The Administration of Palestine is required, under Article 6 of the Mandate, "while ensuring that the rights and position of other sections of the population are not prejudiced," to encourage "close settlement by Jews on the land," and no restriction has been imposed hitherto on the transfer of land from Arabs to Jews. The Reports of several expert Commissions have indicated that, owing to the natural growth of the Arab population and the steady sale in recent years of Arab land to Jews, there is now in certain areas no room for further transfers of Arab land, whilst in some other areas such transfers of land must be restricted if Arab cultivators are to maintain their existing standard of life and a considerable landless Arab population is not soon to be created. In these circumstances, the High Commissioner will be given general powers to prohibit and regulate transfers of land. These powers will date from the publication of this statement of policy and the High Commissioner will retain them throughout the transitional period. . . .

— Reading No. 6 —

OBSERVATIONS OF THE PERMANENT MANDATES COMMISSION ON THE POLICY LAID DOWN IN THE WHITE PAPER OF MAY, 1939[6]

The Mandates Commission was charged with the tasks of examining the reports of the Mandatories and of advising the League Council on all matters relating to the observance of the Mandates. The following are its Observations on the policy of the White Paper of 1939.

✓ ✓ ✓

9. From the first, one fact forced itself to the notice of the Commission—namely, that the policy set out in the White Paper was not in accordance with the interpretation which, in agreement with the mandatory Power and the Council, the Commission had always placed upon the Palestine mandate. . . .

11. The Commission did not, however, confine itself to establishing this single fact. It went on to consider whether the Palestine mandate might not perhaps be open to a new interpretation which, while still respecting its main principles, would be sufficiently flexible for the policy of the White Paper not to appear at variance with it. . . .

12. During the examination of this latter question, divergent views were found to exist among the members of the Commission.

14. . . . four of the latter did not feel able to state that the policy of the White Paper was in conformity with the mandate, any contrary conclusion appearing to them to be ruled out by the very terms of the mandate and by the fundamental intentions of its authors.

[6] League of Nations, Permanent Mandates Commission, *Minutes of the 36th Session* (held at Geneva, June 8-29, 1939), pp. 274-275.

15. The other members, three in number, were unable to share this opinion; they consider that existing circumstances would justify the policy of the White Paper, provided the Council did not oppose it. . . .

— Reading No. 7 —

PALESTINE LAND TRANSFERS REGULATIONS, FEBRUARY 28, 1940[7]

The restriction on Arab land sales to Jews was one of the principles enunciated by the White Paper of 1939. A majority of the Mandates Commission believed that the new British policy violated the Mandate, and even the minority, which thought that it might be justified by existing circumstances, added the condition, "provided the Council did not oppose it." The outbreak of war prevented any action by the Council of the League of Nations. However, the British Government severely curtailed Jewish immigration and issued the following restrictions on land sales.

✓   ✓   ✓

. . . 1. These regulations may be cited as the Land Transfers Regulations, 1940, and shall be deemed to have come into force on the eighteenth day of May, 1939.

2. For the purpose of these regulations there shall be two zones in Palestine which shall be demarcated as set out in the Schedule hereto. . . .

3. The transfer of land situated within Zone A, save to a Palestinian Arab, shall be prohibited. . . .

4. The transfer of land situated within Zone B by a Palestinian Arab, save to a Palestinian Arab, shall be

prohibited unless the person to whom such transfer is intended to be made has received the approval in writing of the High Commissioner, which he may, in his unfettered discretion, grant or refuse. . . .

5. Any transfer of land made in contravention of the provisions of these regulations shall be null and void.

6. —(1) The High Commissioner may require any person making application for the High Commissioner's approval to the transfer of any land under these regulations to support such application by affidavits by himself or any other person.

(2) Any person (*a*) who knowingly makes any false statement in any affidavit made for the purposes of these regulations, or (*b*) who knowingly uses for the purposes of these regulations any affidavit containing any false statement, is guilty of an offense and is liable to imprisonment for seven years. . . .

9. For the purposes of these regulations—

"Palestinian Arab" shall be deemed to be an Arab who is ordinarily resident in Palestine. In case of any dispute as to whether a person is an Arab or whether he is ordinarily resident in Palestine, the question shall be referred to the High Commissioner, whose decision thereon shall be final;

"land" includes water, buildings, trees and any interest in, or right in, to or over land, water, buildings or trees;

"transfer" includes leases, mortgages, charges and any other dispositions.

— Reading No. 8 —

IMMIGRATION STATISTICS [8]

[8] State of Israel, *Government Year-Book,* 5713 (1952), pp. 238, 243, 300, 319. See also D. Gurevich, and A. Gertz, *Statistical Handbook of Jewish Palestine,* 1947 (published by Department of Statistics, Jewish Agency for Palestine, Jerusalem, 1947), pp. 90, 102-103. For Table B, see State of Israel, Central Bureau of Statistics, *Statistical Bulletin of Israel* (English summary), February, 1958, p. 52.

The following imigration statistics are not quite complete. For the years prior to World War I, when the Turks ruled Palestine, only rough estimates are available. The figures of the British administration (1919-1948) are reliable, but they do not include some 31,000 illegal Jewish immigrants.

✓ ✓ ✓

A. IMMIGRATION OF JEWS INTO PALESTINE, 1882-1948

YEARS	NUMBER OF JEWISH IMMIGRANTS
1882-1903	20,000 to 30,000
1904-1914	35,000 to 40,000
1919-1948 (Jan. 1-May 14, 1948)	452,077
1919	1,806
1920	8,223
1921	8,294
1922	8,685
1923	8,175
1924	13,892
1925	34,386
1926	13,855
1927	3,034
1928	2,178
1929	5,249
1930	4,944
1931	4,075
1932	9,553
1933	30,327
1934	42,359
1935	61,854
1936	29,727
1937	10,536
1938	12,868
1939	27,561
1940	8,398
1941	5,886
1942	3,733
1943	8,507
1944	14,464
1945	13,121
1946	17,761
1947	21,542
1948 (Jan. 1-May 14)	17,084

B. ANNUAL IMMIGRATION INTO ISRAEL, MAY 15, 1948-1957

YEAR	IMMIGRATION
1948 (May 15-December 31)	101,825
1949	239,424
1950	169,720
1951	174,014
1952	23,408
1953	10,388
1954	17,485
1955	36,327
1956	54,996
1957	71,100
Total immigration, May 15, 1948-1957	898,687

— Reading No. 9 —

POPULATION STATISTICS[9]

Table A provides census figures (where indicated) and estimates of the British authorities in Palestine. They do not include some 31,000 Jews who entered and remained in Palestine illegally.

✓   ✓   ✓

A. GROWTH OF JEWISH POPULATION IN PALESTINE, 1882-1948

YEAR	JEWS	TOTAL POPULATION	PERCENTAGE OF JEWS IN TOTAL POPULATION
1882	24,000	—	
1890	47,000	—	

[9] *Statistical Handbook of Jewish Palestine,* 1947, cited, pp. 46-47. See also State of Israel, *Government Year-Book,* 5713 (1952), pp. 243, 300. For Table B, see *Statistical Bulletin of Israel,* cited, February, 1958, p. 49.

1900	50,000	—	
1914	85,000	—	
1916-1918	56,700	—	
1922 (census)	83,790	752,048	11.1
1925	121,725	847,238	14.4
1928	151,656	935,951	16.2
1931 (census)	174,610	1,033,314	16.9
1934	282,975	1,210,554	23.4
1937	395,836	1,401,794	28.2
1940	463,535	1,544,530	30.0
1943	502,912	1,676,571	30.0
1945	554,329	1,810,037	30.6
May 14, 1948	c. 650,000	—	

B. POPULATION OF ISRAEL, 1948-1957
(ESTIMATES)

END OF YEAR	TOTAL POPULATION	JEWS	NON-JEWS
1948	879,000	758,702	120,000
1949	1,173,871	1,013,871	160,000
1950	1,370,094	1,202,993	167,101
1951	1,577,825	1,404,392	173,433
1952	1,629,519	1,450,217	179,302
1953	1,669,417	1,483,641	185,776
1954	1,717,814	1,526,009	191,805
1955	1,789,075	1,590,519	198,556
1956	1,872,390	1,667,455	204,935
1957	1,975,954	1,672,741	213,213

ECONOMIC GROWTH[10]

A. GROWTH OF JEWISH INDUSTRY AND HANDICRAFTS, 1925-1943

	INDUSTRY						HANDICRAFTS		
	1925	1930	1933	1937	1943	1946	1930	1933	1937
Number of establishments	536	624	970	1,556	2,120	2,500	1,851	2,418	4,050
Personnel (owners and workers)	4,894	7,582	14,419	21,964	45,049	47,000	3,386	5,176	8,022
Value of annual output (in £P)[a]	—	2,080,000	4,630,000	7,892,000	36,287,000	44,000,000	431,000	722,000	1,217,000
Capital (in £P)[a]	1,517,000	2,095,000	5,097,000	11,064,000	20,523,000	—	139,000	274,000	573,000
Horsepower	5,733	9,932	49,822	104,866	167,532	—	136	713	1,629
Use of electric power (in kwh)	—	—	—	20,300,000	—	74,500,000	—	—	—

[a] The figures for annual output and capital are not entirely comparable because of the variation in the value of the Palestine pound.

[10] The sources for Table A are the *Statistical Handbook of Jewish Palestine, 1947*, cited, pp. 220-221, and the *Hebrew Encyclopedia*, Vol. VI (Jerusalem, 1957), p. 901. See also A. Bonné, *State and Economics in the Middle East* (2nd ed., London, 1955), p. 303. No census of handicrafts was taken in 1943.

B. COMPARATIVE DATA ON MIDDLE EASTERN COUNTRIES[10a]

	EGYPT	SYRIA AND LEBANON	IRAQ	TURKEY	TOTAL	PALESTINE ARABS	PALESTINE JEWS
Density of traffic—							
Number of motor vehicles per 10,000 persons (1938)	21	30	19	6	62	—	—
Railway lines—							
Length in km. per 10,000 persons (1938)	3.1	3.9	3.3	4.2	5.2	—	—
Import per head in £ (average 1935-8)	2.19	1.84	2.83	1.07	10.52	4.07	24.85
Export per head in £ (average 1936-8)	2.10	0.95	1.16	1.21	3.60	2.60	8.73
Volume of foreign trade	4.29	2.79	3.99	2.28	14.12	6.67	33.58
National income in £ per head (1936)	12	13	10	19	26	16	46
State finance (1938-9)—							
Revenue in £ per head	2.323	0.894	2.119	3.286	3.958	2.6	12.1
Expenditure in £ per head	2.494	0.788	2.198	2.958	3.870	—	—
Agricultural productivity in £ (net)—							
Per male earner (1934-5)	18	19.6	18.6	21.8	35.4	29.6	74.2
Per hectare cultivated land in £	25.6	8	8.6	8.2	7.8	—	—
Density of population (1939)—							
Per sq. km. total area	16.7	18.8	8.16	22.9	55.6	—	—
Per sq. km. cultivable area	490	62.7	40.2	58.3	125.1	—	—
Import of machinery, apparatus, electrical goods—							
Per capita average, 1936-8 in £	0.156	0.111	0.254	0.160	0.770	—	—

10a. This Table was taken with permission from A. Bonné, *State and Economics in the Middle East*, cited, p. 221.

— Reading No. 11 —

THE IDEAL OF *HALUTZIUT* OR DEDICATED PIONEERING [11]

In the following excerpt, Ben Gurion eloquently defines halutziut *as a function of human liberty, social equality, and public spirit.*

✓   ✓   ✓

. . . Only with the powerful aid of science can we dispel the destitution and neglect of this Land and withstand the impact of its near and distant environs. We must apply our finest minds to scientific discovery and innovation, uphold the hegemony of science and set its mark on all we do.

But that is not all—there must be the pioneer spirit. By science, man governs nature; by halutziuth, himself. Science serves the needs of humanity, good or evil; halutziuth awakens the dormant strength of will and mind, the sleeping soul of man, and guides them in a new flowering to ends that ethics and history discern. Science is a mighty instrument and does wonders, but it is blind and subject, docile as clay in the potter's hands. Halutziuth charts the actions of man, judicially it measures their spiritual content and inspires him to his highest flights. It unites his intellectual and moral greatness and makes him even greater. It will not compromise or yield, it will not despair; it does not bow down to circumstances. It challenges and rebels, it dares and it transforms, it sees coming events, and perfection is its aim. It alters the present for the sake not of today's wants, but of generations to come, not to gratify the individual but for the common good, not for personal gain but to profit all so-

[11] D. Ben Gurion, *Rebirth and Destiny of Israel* (New York, 1954), pp. 270-272.

ciety and each member of it. It makes every scientist a saint, every man a giant.

Halutziuth will not recognize the conventional grouping of men into a talented elite, the thinkers and leaders, on one hand, and the colorless clay of lesser mortals on the other. As in nature, so in man are concealed forces and skills whereof little has yet come to light, unplumbed depths of impulse and ambition, dynamic aptitudes waiting for release and the stimulus of creating. . . .

. . . Halutziuth elects the line of greatest resistance, to make its triumph the greater. Heroism is not the monopoly of a few, but the gift of every man who would use it. . . . There are no peaks to which man cannot climb, no handicap he cannot surmount—that is the simple, proven faith of halutziuth: its first commandment is to defy circumstances and facts, to refashion our lives as our historic vision bids.

It is a product of human liberty. Its outpourings are willed by self-control, that checks impulses or heightens them, that draws creativeness and courage from the wellsprings of the soul. Without freedom we cannot discipline ourselves. A robot cannot be a pioneer, for he patterns his life to others' designs, a decadent personification of submission, impotent over his own desires and thoughts. A robot can do great things, like any lifeless machine, but only in the hands of a skilled engineer. He is no creator, but raw stuff. The pioneer makes his own life and his friends'.

And man must be equal, to be pioneer. Where discrimination is rife and creation only for a favored few, the fountain of halutziuth is choked and runs dry. Only where men are peers does the rich fountain flow of man's secret worth. And last, the cooperation of man is necessary: his trust in society, an attachment to his fellows, a will to unity.

Halutziuth is service to commonalty, that is its beginning and its end. . . .

— Reading No. 12 —

SOURCES OF JEWISH SOCIAL IDEALISM[12]

From hoary antiquity, the vision of a moral order per-meated the thought and affected the practice of Judaism. Ethical constraints were interposed between the privileged and the strong, on the one hand, and the weak, unfortu-nate and the defenseless on the other. The exercises of power—political, economic or social—was to be curbed by the requirements of justice, kindness and humility, for all human life had sanctity and might did not sanction the degradation of human personality or the employment of one man as the instrument of another.

In this stream of ethical idealism, the current of what we call today social justice was always evident. In Bibli-cal times, the perennial plaint was against oppression and exploitation, against the urge to dominate and the lust for gain. The positive injunctions—to surrender the gleanings of the field, to protect the widow, the fatherless and the stranger, to deal justly with the hired servant, not to betray the fugitive slave—were actuated not only by the spirit of charity but also by a human regard for the feel-ings of the objects of charity.

Benevolence and charity became functioning ideals among Jews wherever they dwelt, and philanthropy (*zedakah*) an obligatory form of religious practice; in-deed, a symbol of righteousness. The emphasis, at least in precept, was upon anonymous giving so that generosity would not be tarnished by a display of wealth and power. And the most meritorious benefaction was that form of assistance which enabled the poor to help themselves.

This preoccupation with poverty and with the humilia-tions attendant upon economic inequality and inferior social status was reinforced in the Jewish heritage by a yearning for human freedom and equality. The ideals of

[12] From a manuscript by the author of this book.

the fatherhood of God and brotherhood of man were proclaimed with passion by the Hebrew prophets and expounded and elucidated by Rabbis and sages in countless homilies and maxims. Nor did these ideals remain purely precept. The equitable distribution of property was a living issue in Biblical times. Freedom to differ within the confines of basic religious premises was recognized and, on the whole, tolerated in Talmudic and later periods. And labor—physical toil in the field or in the artisan's shop—was not only commended for the masses but also esteemed as a proper means of self-support for the religious and intellectual leaders, the Rabbis.

Nineteenth-century Europe witnessed a struggle between liberalism and reaction, and in this struggle the overwhelming majority of Europe's Jews espoused the liberal cause. There were, of course, compelling political and economic motivations for the liberal inclinations of the Jews, but the social idealism of Jewish tradition must not be ruled out as a factor.

Similarly, the socialistic theories of the latter half of the nineteenth century attracted an element among the Jewish intellectuals, especially in Eastern Europe. As a rule, Jews who espoused socialism were "assimilationists," that is, they rejected Jewish nationalism and looked to the socialist revolution and reconstruction to solve the Jewish problem. Early in the twentieth century, however, a synthesis of Zionism and socialism was attempted, and Labor Zionist groupings emerged. Labor Zionism struck deep roots in Palestine and played an important role in the development of the National Home. And in Labor Zionism, the ideals of social justice, which formed so vital a part of the Jewish heritage, emerged as guiding principles for practical action.

Finally, the fact that so many of the early Jewish settlers in Palestine were emigrants from Czarist Russia had an important bearing on the subject. The ancient prophets had been wont to remind their hearers of the bondage in Egypt: "Remember that thou wast a slave in the land of Egypt" had been a refrain apparently of telling effect in denunciations of economic or political oppression. The fugitives from the Czarist inferno needed no reminder of Russian oppressions and humiliations. These had seared their minds and bodies and instilled a hatred of political tyranny and economic exploitation. It was the men and women of the Second *Aliya* (wave of immigration), set in motion by the Kishenev pogrom (1903) and the failure of the Russian Revolution of 1905, who initiated the novel communal type of agricultural settlement. These idealists were determined to build a new life in Palestine free of the insecurities and inequalities of the Russian ghettoes, a life founded on self-labor, freedom, equality, and cooperation.

— Reading No. 13 —

REVIVAL OF HEBREW AS A LIVING LANGUAGE [13]

ESTIMATED NUMBERS AND PERCENTAGES OF PERSONS USING HEBREW IN THE JEWISH POPULATION (1914-54)

	Estimate for the end of Turkish Period (1914)	Census at the end of Mandatory Period (Nov. 1948)	Estimate after 2½ years of mass immigration (Dec. 1950)	Estimate based on Labour Force Survey (June 1954)
No. speaking Hebrew as "only" or "first" language (aged 2 or more)	34,000 [a]	511,000 [c]	679,000	861,100
Same per 100 persons aged 2 or more	About 40% [b]	75.1% [c]	About 60%	60.9%
aged 2-14	53.7%	93.4%	80.3%	83.9% [e]
aged 15 or more	25.6%	69.5%	52.0%	52.8% [f]
Index of use of Hebrew: At all ages	?	71.1	?	57.7
At ages 2-14	?	90.9 [d]	?	80.5 [e]
At ages 15 or more	?	65.0	?	49.7 [f]

[a] All ages.
[b] All ages over 1.
[c] Persons aged 2 or more—multiplied by 75.1, which is the over-all percentage of Hebrew-speaking obtained over all persons stating use of language. (For most children under 2 no data on use of language were reported. These children constituted the great majority among persons with no data on use of languages.)
[d] All "stated" under 15 years of age (see preceding note).
[e] Per 100 aged 2-13.
[f] Per 100 aged 14 and more.

[13] Source of table: R. Bachi, "A Statistical Analysis of the Revival of Hebrew in Israel," *Scripta Hierosolymitana*, III (Jerusalem, 1956, The Magnes Press, Hebrew University), p. 193. See also *Statistical Abstract of Israel*, No. 8, 1956-1957, p. 243. The latter source indicates that by June, 1956, 58.4% of Jews aged 14 and over spoke Hebrew as their only or main language.

— Reading No. 14 —

THE MEANING OF *ALIYA*[14]

Berl Katznelson (1887-1944) was one of the most influential leaders of the Histadrut. He was born in Russia and settled in Palestine in 1909. He worked as an agricultural laborer, was a member of a collective, devoted himself to labor organization and to cultural efforts among workers, and was recognized as a foremost ideologist of the labor movement. He was a founder of the Histadrut and served as the editor of Davar, *its daily newspaper. The following excerpt expresses his conception of Aliya.*

↗   ↗   ↗

There are many meanings to the word *"Aliyah."* *"Aliyah"* means climbing the rungs of a ladder, and it also means going to Palestine. Going to any other land we call "Immigration," but returning to Zion, and to Zion alone, is *"Aliyah."* *"Aliyah"* is a rise from the depths of the *Galuth* to the homeland, to the land of liberty. We use *Aliyah* in both the material and the spiritual sense. There is an *Aliyah* of will and of hope. There is an *Aliyah* of the class and of the nation, and there is also an *Aliyah* of the individual. We have always looked upon ourselves as *Halutzim*, the pioneers of the people. Behind us, thousands await redemption. They shall come, and, together with us, shall build this land.

[14] Quoted in A. Revusky, *The Histadrut: A Labor Commonwealth in the Making* (New York, 1938), pp. 27-28.

— Reading No. 15 —

AARON DAVID GORDON AND THE IDEALIZATION OF LABOR [15]

As is often the case with lofty ideals, the consecration of labor to the regeneration of land and people became identified with an individual. Aaron David Gordon (1856-1922) was a symbol of labor idealism.

Born in southwest Russia, Gordon received a thorough traditional Jewish education, to which he added considerable secular knowledge, including proficiency in several languages. His livelihood was earned with ease as a minor official on the estate of a wealthy kinsman, and he lived the honored life of an intellectual about whom the cultural life of his community revolved. But he was troubled in spirit because of the unwholesome life of the Jews about him. In 1904, at the age of forty-eight, he left home and family to begin life anew as a laborer in Palestine, and several years thereafter, he played a leading role in the establishment of Dagania, the celebrated cooperative settlement.

The ideal of work struck Gordon with the force of overpowering truth, and it became at once an article of faith and a philosophy of life. More, self-labor was a gospel of salvation, promising personal and national redemption. Gordon felt the compulsion to communicate his revelation, and in numerous essays, articles, letters, and fragments he taught and preached his cardinal principles, namely, to return to the soil and to nature, to reclaim the land by manual labor, and to redeem the human and national spirit by contact and communion with nature. His writings were published in Hebrew in five volumes, and a selection is available in English in his Selected Essays. *The spiritual intensity of this man's faith in work is revealed in the following passage.*

[15] A. D. Gordon, *Selected Essays* (trans. by F. Burnce; New York: League for Labor Palestine, 1938), pp. 247-251.

↗   ↗   ↗

And when, O Man, you will return to Nature, you
will open your eyes on that day and you will gaze straight
into the eyes of Nature, you will see therein your own
image, and you will know that you have returned to your-
self. . . .

On that day, O Man, a new spirit will be given you;
you will experience a new sensation, a new hunger . . .
for work. You will derive pleasure from every task that
you undertake, from every deed that you do. . . . You
will set your heart to work, to any work, any task amid
nature, amid the universal expanse. . . .

Then when you will perform your work, the expanse
of the universe will be to you a vast shop, and you and
Nature the workers. One heart and one spirit will animate
both of you. . . . You will certainly have moments in
which seemingly your whole being melts into the infinite.
Then you will grow silent. . . . You will sense that
which cannot be expressed except by work; you will labor
with all your strength, mightily, joyously. And you will
hear a tiny voice rise from your task and say: "Work, O
Man, each one of you, work."

— Reading No. 16 —

PRELIMINARY REPORT TO THE PRESIDENT ON DISPLACED PERSONS IN GERMANY AND AUSTRIA (THE HARRISON REPORT), AUGUST, 1945 [16]

In June, 1945, President Truman instructed Earl G. Harrison, the American representative on the Intergovernmental Committee on Refugees to inquire into and report on the condition of displaced persons situated especially in Germany and Austria. He was directed to give particular attention to the problems and needs of Jewish refugees and to their views as to their future destinations. The following excerpts portray the wretched condition of the Jewish refugees and include the recommendations for their settlement in Palestine.

✓   ✓   ✓

I

GERMANY AND AUSTRIA: CONDITIONS

(1) Generally speaking, three months after V-E Day, and even longer after the liberation of individual groups, many Jewish displaced persons and other possibly non-repatriables are living under guard behind barbed-wire fences in camps of several descriptions (built by the Germans for slave laborers and Jews), including some of the most notorious of the concentration camps, amid crowded, frequently unsanitary and generally grim conditions, in complete idleness, with no opportunity, except

[16] *The New York Times,* September 30, 1945; *Department of State Bulletin,* XIII (September 30, 1945), pp. 456-463.

surreptitiously, to communicate with the outside world,
waiting, hoping for some word of encouragement and
action in their behalf.

(2) While there has been marked improvement in the
health of survivors of the Nazi starvation and persecution
program, there are many pathetic malnutrition cases both
among the hospitalized and in the general population of
the camps. The death rate has been high since liberation,
as was to be expected. One Army chaplain, a Rabbi,
personally attended, since liberation, 23,000 burials (90
per cent Jews) at Berger Belsen alone, one of the largest
and most vicious of the concentration camps, where, incidentally, despite persistent reports to the contrary,
14,000 displaced persons are still living, including over
7,000 Jews. . . .

(3) Although some camp commandants have man-
aged, in spite of the many obvious difficulties, to find
clothing of one kind or another for their charges, many
of the Jewish displaced persons, late in July, had no
clothing other than their concentration camp garb—a
rather hideous striped pajama effect—while others, to
their chagrin, were obliged to wear German SS uniforms.
It is questionable which clothing they hate the more. . . .

(5) The most absorbing worry of these Nazi and war
victims concerns relatives—wives, husbands, parents, children. Most of them have been separated for three, four
or five years and they cannot understand why the lib-
erators should not have undertaken immediately the
organized effort to reunite family groups. . . .

II

NEEDS OF THE JEWS

While it is impossible to state accurately the number of
Jews now in that part of Germany not under Russian occupation, all indications point to the fact that the number
is small, with 100,000 probably the top figure. . . .

The first and plainest need of these people is a recognition of their actual status and by this I mean their status
as Jews . . . Refusal to recognize the Jews as such has
the effect, in this situation, of closing one's eyes to their
former and more barbaric persecution, which has already
made them a separate group with greater needs.

Their second great need can be presented only by discussing what I found to be their wishes as to future destinations.

For reasons that are obvious and need not be labored, most Jews want to leave Germany and Austria as soon as possible. . . . They want to be evacuated to Palestine now. . . . Palestine is definitely and preeminently the first choice. . . .

IV

CONCLUSIONS AND RECOMMENDATIONS

. . . Specifically, in the days immediately ahead, the Jews in Germany and Austria should have the first claim upon the conscience of the people of the United States and Great Britain. . . .

In this connection, the issue of Palestine must be faced. . . . To anyone who has visited the concentration camps and who has talked with the despairing survivors, it is nothing short of calamitous to contemplate that the gates of Palestine should be soon closed. . . .

In conclusion, I wish to repeat that the main solution, in many ways the only real solution, of the problem lies in the quick evacuation of all non-repatriable Jews in Germany and Austria, who wish it, to Palestine. . . .

The civilized world owes it to this handful of survivors to provide them with a home where they can again settle down and begin to live as human beings.

— Reading No. 17 —

LETTER FROM PRESIDENT TRUMAN TO PRIME MINISTER ATTLEE, AUGUST 31, 1945 [17]

Department of State Bulletin, XIII (November 18, 1945), pp. 790-791.

The Harrison Report (see Reading No. 16) *crystallized American public opinion in favor of the settlement of Jewish refugees in Palestine. It was endorsed by President Truman, who addressed the following letter to the Prime Minister of the United Kingdom.*

✓   ✓   ✓

My Dear Mr. Prime Minister:

Because of the natural interest of this Government in the present condition and future fate of those displaced persons in Germany who may prove to be stateless or non-repatriable, we recently sent Mr. Earl G. Harrison to inquire into the situation. . . .

Instructions were given to Mr. Harrison to inquire particularly into the problems and needs of the Jewish refugees among the displaced persons. . . .

I have now received his report. In view of our conversations at Potsdam I am sure that you will find certain portions of the report interesting. I am, therefore, sending you a copy.

I should like to call your attention to the conclusions and recommendations appearing on Page 8 and the following pages—especially the references to Palestine. It appears that the available certificates for immigration to Palestine will be exhausted in the near future. It is suggested that the granting of an additional one hundred thousand of such certificates would contribute greatly to a sound solution for the future of Jews still in Germany and Austria, and for other Jewish refugees who do not wish to remain where they are or who for understandable reasons do not desire to return to their countries of origin.

On the basis of this and other information which has come to me I concur in the belief that no other single matter is so important for those who have known the horrors of concentration camps for over a decade as is the future of immigration possibilities into Palestine. The number of such persons who wish immigration to Palestine or who would qualify for admission there is, unfortunately, no longer as large as it was before the Nazis began their extermination program. As I said to you in Potsdam, the American people, as a whole, firmly believe that immigration into Palestine should not be closed and that a reasonable number of Europe's persecuted Jews should, in accordance with their wishes, be permitted to resettle there.

I know you are in agreement on the proposition that future peace in Europe depends in large measure upon our finding sound solutions of problems confronting the displaced and formerly persecuted groups of people. No claim is more meritorious than that of the groups who for so many years have known persecution and enslavement.

The main solution appears to lie in the quick evacuation of as many as possible of the non-repatriable Jews, who wish it, to Palestine. If it is to be effective, such action should not be long delayed.

Very sincerely yours,
HARRY S. TRUMAN

— Reading No. 18 —

CONCURRENT CONGRESSIONAL RESOLUTION, DECEMBER, 1945 [18]

During and immediately after World War II, American public opinion was strongly in favor of Jewish aspirations in Palestine. On November 2, 1942, a supporting declaration was signed by a majority of the members of the Senate and by nearly 200 members of the House of Representatives. In 1944 the Democratic and Republican National Conventions vigorously supported Jewish demands. On July 2, 1945, a majority of the members of both houses of Congress addressed a letter to the President, calling upon him to press for the establishment of a democratic Jewish Commonwealth in Palestine, as well as for unrestricted Jewish immigration. A petition of the

[18] *U.S., Statutes at Large, vol. 59, pp. 848-849.*

same date and of similar content was addressed to the President and signed by the governors of forty states of the United States. Finally, the following Concurrent Resolution was passed by the Senate on December 17 and by the House on December 19, 1945.

✓   ✓   ✓

CONCURRENT RESOLUTIONS

WHEREAS the Sixty-seventh Congress of the United States on June 30, 1922, unanimously resolved "That the United States of America favors the establishment in Palestine of a national home for the Jewish people, it being clearly understood that nothing shall be done which may prejudice the civil and religious rights of Christian and all other non-Jewish communities in Palestine, and that the holy places and religious buildings and sites in Palestine shall be adequately protected"; and

WHEREAS the ruthless persecution of the Jewish people in Europe has clearly demonstrated the need for a Jewish homeland as a haven for the large numbers who have become homeless as a result of this persecution; and

WHEREAS these urgent necessities are evidenced by the President's request for the immediate right of entry into Palestine of one hundred thousand additional Jewish refugees; . . . .

THEREFORE BE IT

Resolved by the Senate (the House of Representatives concurring), That the interest shown by the President in the solution of this problem is hereby commended and that the United States shall use its good offices with the mandatory power to the end that Palestine shall be opened for free entry of Jews into that country to the maximum of its agricultural and economic potentialities, and that there shall be full opportunity for colonization and development, so that they may freely proceed with the upbuilding of Palestine as the Jewish national home and, in association with all elements of the population, establish Palestine as a democratic commonwealth in which all men, regardless of race or creed, shall have equal rights.

— Reading No. 19 —

RECOMMENDATIONS OF THE ANGLO-AMERICAN COMMITTEE OF INQUIRY ON PALESTINE, APRIL 20, 1946—EXTRACTS [19]

The Anglo-American Committee of Inquiry was set up in November-December, 1945, in the hope of finding a formula that would harmonize American and British policies on Palestine. The Committee held hearings in Washington, London, Palestine, Cairo, and other Arab centers of the Middle East, and its members visited Jewish displaced persons camps in Europe. It submitted an extensive report, including the following recommendations.

✓ ✓ ✓

Recommendation No. 1. We have to report that such information as we received about countries other than Palestine gave no hope of substantial assistance in finding homes for Jews wishing or impelled to leave Europe.

But Palestine alone cannot meet the emigration needs of the Jewish victims of Nazi and Fascist persecution; the whole world shares responsibility for them and indeed for the resettlement of all "displaced persons". . . .

Recommendation No. 2. We recommend (*a*) that 100,-000 certificates be authorized immediately for the admission into Palestine of Jews who have been the victims of Nazi and Fascist persecution; (*b*) that these certificates be awarded as far as possible in 1946 and that actual immigration be pushed forward as rapidly as conditions will permit. . . .

[19] Anglo-American Committee of Inquiry, *Report to the United States Government and His Majesty's Government in the United Kingdom* (Dept. of State, Publication No. 2536), Chap. I, pp. 1-12.

Recommendation No. 3. In order to dispose, once and for all, of the exclusive claims of Jews and Arabs to Palestine, we regard it as essential that a clear statement of the following principles should be made: I. That Jew shall not dominate Arab and Arab shall not dominate Jew in Palestine. II. That Palestine shall be neither a Jewish state nor an Arab state. . . .

Recommendation No. 4. We have reached the conclusion that . . . now and for some time to come, any attempt to establish either an independent Palestinian State or independent Palestinian States would result in civil strife such as might threaten the peace of the world. . . .

Recommendation No. 5. . . . we recommend that the mandatory or trustee should proclaim the principle that Arab economic, educational and political advancement in Palestine is of equal importance with that of the Jews; and should at once prepare measures designed to bridge the gap which now exists and raise the Arab standard of living to that of the Jews. . . .

Recommendation No. 6. We recommend that, pending the early reference to the United Nations and the execution of a trusteeship agreement, the mandatory should administer Palestine according to the mandate which declares with regard to immigration that "The administration of Palestine, while ensuring that the rights and position of other sections of the population are not prejudiced shall facilitate Jewish immigration under suitable conditions". . . .

Recommendation No. 7. (*a*) We recommend that the Land Transfers Regulations of 1940 be rescinded and replaced by regulations based on a policy of freedom in the sale, lease or use of land, irrespective of race, community or creed, and providing adequate protection for the interests of small owners and tenant cultivators; (*b*) We further recommend that steps be taken to render nugatory and to prohibit provisions in conveyances, leases and agreements relating to land which stipulate that only members of one race, community or creed may be employed on or about or in connection therewith. . . .

Recommendation No. 9. We recommend that . . . the educational system of both Jews and Arabs be reformed including the introduction of compulsory education within a reasonable time. . . .

Recommendation No. 10. We recommend that, if this Report is adopted, it should be made clear beyond all doubt to both Jews and Arabs that any attempt from either side, by threats of violence, by terrorism, or by the organization or use of illegal armies to prevent its execution, will be resolutely suppressed.

Furthermore, we express the view that the Jewish Agency should at once resume active cooperation with the Mandatory in the suppression of terrorism and of illegal immigration. . . .

— Reading No. 20 —

UNITED NATIONS GENERAL ASSEMBLY RESOLUTION ON THE PARTITION OF PALESTINE, NOVEMBER 29, 1947: RESOLUTION 181 (II)— EXTRACTS[20]

The resolution adopted by the General Assembly provided for the partition of Palestine into an Arab state, a Jewish state, and an enclave of the City of Jerusalem and its environs to be under a special international regime. The economic union of Palestine was to be preserved, and detailed provision was made for the delimitation of boundaries, for the Holy Places, for democratic elections and religious and minority rights, and for the peaceful and orderly transfer of authority through the agency of a United Nations Palestine Commission.

The Palestine Arabs and the Arab states rejected the recommendations and resorted to force to prevent implementation. The British, as Mandatory, likewise refused to cooperate with the United Nations Palestine Commis-

[20] United Nations, *Official Records of the Second Session of the General Assembly, Resolutions* (16 September-29 November, 1947), pp. 131-150.

sion. *The partition of Palestine was effected through armed conflict.*

✓   ✓   ✓

PLAN OF PARTITION
WITH ECONOMIC UNION

Future Constitution and Government of Palestine

1. The Mandate for Palestine shall terminate as soon as possible but in any case not later than August 1, 1948.

2. The armed forces of the Mandatory Power shall be progressively withdrawn from Palestine, the withdrawal to be completed as soon as possible but in any case not later than August 1, 1948. . . .

The Mandatory Power shall use its best endeavors to ensure that an area situated in the territory of the Jewish State, including a seaport and hinterland adequate to provide facilities for a substantial immigration, shall be evacuated at the earliest possible date and in any event not later than February 1, 1948.

3. Independent Arab and Jewish States and the Special International Regime for the City of Jerusalem, set forth in . . . this Plan, shall come into existence in Palestine two months after the evacuation of the armed forces of the Mandatory Power has been completed but in any case not later than October 1, 1948. . . .

Steps Preparatory to Independence

1. A Commission shall be set up consisting of one representative of each of five Member States. . . .

2. The administration of Palestine shall, as the Mandatory Power withdraws its armed forces, be progressively turned over to the Commission. . . .

3. On its arrival in Palestine the Commission shall proceed to carry out measures for the establishment of the frontiers of the Arab and Jewish States and the City of Jerusalem in accordance with the general lines of the recommendations of the General Assembly on the partition of Palestine. . . .

4. The Commission, after consultation with the democratic parties and other public organizations of the Arab and Jewish States, shall select and establish in each State as rapidly as possible a Provisional Council of Govern-

ment. The activities of both the Arab and Jewish Provisional Councils of Government shall be carried out under the general direction of the Commission. . . .

6. The Provisional Council of Government of each State, acting under the Commission, shall progressively receive from the Commission full responsibility for the administration of that State in the period between the termination of the Mandate and the establishment of the States' independence.

8. The Provisional Council of Government of each State shall, within the shortest time possible, recruit an armed militia from the residents of that State. . . .

This armed militia in each State shall, for operational purposes, be under the command of Jewish or Arab officers resident in that State, but general political and military control, including the choice of the militia's High Command, shall be exercised by the Commission.

9. The Provisional Council of Government of each State shall, not later than two months after the withdrawal of the armed forces of the Mandatory Power, hold elections to the Constituent Assembly which shall be conducted on democratic lines. . . .

10. The Constituent Assembly of each State shall draft a democratic Constitution for its State and choose a provisional government to succeed the Provisional Council of Government appointed by the Commission. . . .

11. The Commission shall appoint a Preparatory Economic Commission of three members to make whatever arrangements are possible for economic cooperation, with a view to establishing, as soon as practicable, the Economic Union and the Joint Economic Board, as provided in section D below. . . .

— Reading No. 21 —

THE FLIGHT OF THE ARABS[21]

[21] Moshe Pearlman, *The Army of Israel* (New York, Philosophical Library, 1950), pp. 116-117.

*The following reports relate to the situation in Haifa.
The British were in control when the Jews captured the
city, and the British District Superintendent of Police
wrote secret reports daily. The documents were found in
the police files by the Haganah. The italics represent un-
derlining added by the author from whose book the
documents are reproduced.*

✓   ✓   ✓

10/PS.

District Police Headquarters,
(C.I.D.)
P.O.B. 700, Haifa
26th April, 1948

SECRET

A/A.I.G., C.I.D.

Subject: General Situation—Haifa District

The situation in Haifa remains unchanged. *Every effort
is being made by the Jews to persuade the Arab populace
to stay and carry on with their normal lives, to get their
shops and businesses open and to be assured that their
lives and interests will be safe.* On the other side the
evacuation goes on and a large road convoy escorted by
Military and containing a large percentage of Christians
left Haifa for Beirut yesterday. An estimated number of
700 has been given for this convoy and evacuation by sea
goes on steadily.

10/PS.

District Police Headquarters . . .
28th April, 1948

SECRET

A/A.I.G., C.I.D.

Subject: General Situation—Haifa District

There is no change in the situation in Haifa. The Jews are *still making every effort to persuade the Arab populace to remain and settle back into their normal lives in the town.* Another convoy left Tireh for Transjordan and the evacuation by sea continues. The quays and harbour are still crowded with refugees and their household effects, all waiting an opportunity to get a place on one of the boats leaving Haifa. Some families have lived and slept on the quaysides for several days waiting a chance to get away. Life in the New Business Centre has returned to normal with all shops and businesses functioning.

The steam trawler "TADORME" renamed the Haganah ship "OPERATION CASTEL" was brought into Haifa harbour at 5.30 A.M. with a total of 559 persons on board made up of 332 males, 182 females and 45 children. The illegals were transferred in the usual manner to the Empire Comfort and the Empire Rest. During the transhipment the illegals twice refused to move from their ship and had to be got on the move again by naval and marine personnel. The transhipment was completed at 11.15 A.M. and the illegals left for Cyprus.

10/PS.

(Sgd.) A. J. Bidmead
for SUPERINTENDENT OF POLICE

District Police Headquarters . . .
26th April, 1948.

SECRET

A/A.I.C., C.I.D.

Subject: General Situation—Haifa District.

Haifa remains quiet. Yesterday produced a noticeable change in the general atmosphere and businesses and shops in the lower town were open for the first time in many days. Traffic started to move normally around the town and people returning to their places of business filled the streets. In fact, Haifa presented a more normal appearance than it had done for a long while. Some Arabs were seen moving among the Jews in the lower town and German Colony area and these were allowed free and unmolested passage. *An appeal has been made to the Arabs by the Jews to reopen their shops and businesses in order to relieve the difficulties of feeding the Arab population. Evacuation was still going on yesterday and several trips were made by 'Z' craft to Acre. Roads, too, were crowded with people leaving Haifa with their belongings. At a meeting yesterday afternoon Arab leaders reiterated their determination to evacuate the entire Arab population and they have been given the loan of ten 3-ton military trucks as from this morning to assist the evacuation.*

Yesterday morning a Jew attempted to pass the drop barrier of Police H.Q. facing Palmers Gate wheeling a barrow. He was shot and killed by a Police sentry.

At 0640 hrs. yesterday Tireh village was again attacked with mortar fire. Casualties and damage not known.

A report has been received from Military to the effect that at 23.50 hrs. yesterday Jews attacked Acre from the direction of Ein Hamifratz and Tall al Fukhkhar. An advance party succeeded in demolishing three houses in the Manshiya Quarter and then heavy mortar fire was directed at the town. Several mortar bombs landed in Acre Prison and all the inmates have escaped. The British warden staff are safe. Military proceeded to the scene and opened fire with artillery on Ein Hamifratz. The Jews thereupon withdrew and a convoy of 11 vehicles was seen proceeding in the direction of Haifa. Casualties to both sides are not known.

(A. J. Bidmead.)
for SUPERINTENDENT OF POLICE.

Copy:— District Commissioner, Haifa.
       Superintendent of Police, Haifa.
       File.

— Reading No. 22 —

THE PROCLAMATION OF INDEPENDENCE, MAY 14, 1948 [22]

The independence of Israel was proclaimed on Friday afternoon (Sabbath Eve), May 14, 1948, at a meeting of the Provisional State Council held in the Tel Aviv Museum. "At four o'clock precisely Ben Gurion, flanked by his twelve fellow Ministers of the new Jewish State, stood up. The small hall was packed with people, with emotion and with history. Ben Gurion, in a blue lounge suit, began to read in a matter-of-fact voice. For five minutes he recalled centuries, tragedies and aspirations in short tense paragraphs that moved like a Greek drama to their predestined climax. . . .

"Ben Gurion paused for a moment. . . . And then in ringing tones [he proclaimed the establishment of Israel]. . . The Proclamation had taken seventeen minutes. . . Immediately after the reading and signature of the Declaration of Independence, Ben Gurion announced the new state's first Government decrees. The British White Paper of 1939 was declared forthwith annulled. The laws restricting Jewish immigration into Palestine and prohibiting the purchase by Jews of land in certain parts of Palestine were abolished and abrogated. . . ." *

* J. Kimche, *Seven Fallen Pillars* (New York, 1953), pp. 236-238.

❦   ❦   ❦

THE LAND OF ISRAEL was the birthplace of the Jewish people. Here their spiritual, religious and national identity was formed. Here they achieved independence and created a culture of national and universal significance. Here they wrote and gave the Bible to the world.

Exiled from the Land of Israel the Jewish people re-

[2] State of Israel, *Government Yearbook*, 5711 (1950), pp. 43-45.

mained faithful to it in all the countries of their dispersion, never ceasing to pray and hope for their return and the restoration of their national freedom. Impelled by this historic association, Jews stove throughout the centuries to go back to the land of their fathers and regain their statehood. In recent decades they returned in their masses. They reclaimed the wilderness, revived their language, built cities and villages, and established a vigorous and ever-growing community, with its own economic and cultural life. They sought peace yet were prepared to defend themselves. They brought the blessings of progress to all inhabitants of the country and looked forward to sovereign independence.

In the year 1897 the First Zionist Congress, inspired by Theodor Herzl's vision of the Jewish State, proclaimed the right of the Jewish people to national revival in their own country.

This right was acknowledged by the Balfour Declaration of November 2, 1917, and re-affirmed by the Mandate of the League of Nations, which gave explicit international recognition to the historic connection of the Jewish people with Palestine and their right to reconstitute their National Home.

The recent holocaust, which engulfed millions of Jews in Europe, proved anew the need to solve the problem of the homelessness and lack of independence of the Jewish people by means of the reestablishment of the Jewish State, which would open the gates to all Jews and endow the Jewish people with equality of status among the family of nations.

The survivors of the disastrous slaughter in Europe, and also Jews from other lands, have not desisted from their efforts to reach Eretz-Yisrael, in face of difficulties, obstacles and perils; and have not ceased to urge their right to a life of dignity, freedom and honest toil in their ancestral land.

In the Second World War the Jewish people in Palestine made their full contribution to the struggle of the freedom-loving nations against the Nazi evil. The sacrifices of their soldiers and their war effort gained them the right to rank with the nations which founded the United Nations.

On November 29, 1947, the General Assembly of the United Nations adopted a Resolution requiring the establishment of a Jewish State in Palestine. The General Assembly called upon the inhabitants of the country to take all the necessary steps on their part to put the plan into effect. This recognition by the United Nations of the right of the Jewish people to establish their independent State is unassailable.

It is the natural right of the Jewish people to lead, as do all other nations, an independent existence in its sovereign State.

ACCORDINGLY WE, the members of the National Council, representing the Jewish people in Palestine and the World Zionist Movement, are met together in solemn assembly today, the day of termination of the British Mandate for Palestine; and by virtue of the natural and historic right of the Jewish people and of the Resolution of the General Assembly of the United Nations.

WE HEREBY PROCLAIM the establishment of the Jewish State in Palestine, to be called Medinath Yisrael (The State of Israel).

WE HEREBY DECLARE that, as from the termination of the Mandate at midnight, the 14th—15th May, 1948, and pending the setting up of the duly elected bodies of the State in accordance with a Constitution, to be drawn up by the Constituent Assembly not later than the 1st October, 1948, the National Council shall act as the Provisional Government of the Jewish State, which shall be known as Israel.

THE STATE OF ISRAEL will be open to the immigration of Jews from all countries of their dispersion; will promote the development of the country for the benefit of all its inhabitants; will be based on the principles of liberty, justice and peace as conceived by the Prophets of Israel; will uphold the full social and political equality of all its citizens, without distinction of religion, race or sex; will guarantee freedom of religion, conscience, education and culture; will safeguard the Holy Places of all religions; and will loyally uphold the principles of the United Nations Charter.

THE STATE OF ISRAEL will be ready to cooperate with the organs and representatives of the United Nations in the implementation of the Resolution of the Assembly of November 29, 1947, and will take steps to bring about the Economic Union over the whole of Palestine.

We appeal to the United Nations to assist the Jewish people in the building of its State and to admit Israel into the family of nations. In the midst of wanton aggression, we yet call upon the Arab inhabitants of the State of Israel to preserve the ways of peace and play their part in the development of the State, on the basis of full and equal citizenship and due representation in all its bodies and institutions—provisional and permanent.

We extend our hand in peace and neighbourliness to all the neighbouring states and their peoples, and invite them to cooperate with the independent Jewish nation for the common good of all. The State of Israel is prepared to make its contribution to the progress of the Middle East as a whole.

Our call goes out to the Jewish people all over the world to rally to our side in the task of immigration and development and to stand by us in the great struggle for the fulfillment of the dream of generations for the redemption of Israel.

With trust in Almighty God, we set our hand to this Declaration, at this Session of the Provisional State Council, on the soil of the Homeland, in the city of Tel Aviv, on this Sabbath eve, the fifth of Iyar, 5708, the fourteenth day of May, 1948.

Signed:

D. Ben Gurion, Daniel Auster, Mordechai Ben Tov, Itzhak Ben Zvi, Eliahu Berlin, P. Bernstein, Rabbi Zeev Gold, Meir Grabovsky, Y. Greenbaum, Abraham Granovsky, Eliahu Dobkin, Meir Vilner, Zorah Warhaftig, Herzl Vardi, Rachel Cohen, Kalman Kahana, S. Kovashi, Itzhak Meir Levin, M. D. Levinstein, Zvi Luria, Golda Myerson, Nahum Nir-Raffalkes, Zvi Segal, Yehuda Leib Hacohen Fishman, David Zvi Pinhas, Aharon Zisling, Moshe Kolodni, E. Kaplan, A. Katzenelson, Felix Rosenblut, D. Remez, B. Repetur, Mordecai Shattner, Ben Zion Sternberg, Bechor Shitreet, Moshe Shapira, Moshe Shertok.

— Reading No. 23 —

THE NATIONAL ELECTIONS[23]

The following table presents a comparative analysis of the three national elections held in Israel, including the participating political parties and factions, the votes polled by each and the mandates secured, the total votes cast, and the percentage of voter participation in the elections. The table is a composite of five tables contained in the source indicated below.

[23] See State of Israel, Central Bureau of Statistics, *Totzaot Habhirot* (Election Results), Special Series, No. 51 (Jerusalem, August, 1956), Tables I-V, pp. 3-7.

PARTIES	FIRST KNESSET ELECTIONS, JANUARY 25, 1949			SECOND ELECTIONS, KNESSET JULY 30, 1951			THIRD KNESSET ELECTIONS, JULY 26, 1955		
	Votes	Percent of total	Members	Votes	Percent of total	Members	Votes	Percent of total	Members
Mapai	155,274	35.7	46	256,456	37.3	45	274,735	32.2	40
Mapam	64,018	14.7	19	86,096	12.5	15	62,401	7.3	9
Ahdut Haavoda-Poalei Zion	—	—	—	—	—	—	69,475	8.2	10
General Zionist	22,861	5.2	7	111,394	16.2	20	87,099	10.2	13
Hapoel Hamizrahi*	52,982	12.2	16	46,347	6.8	8	77,936	9.1	11
Mizrahi*				10,383	1.5	2			
Agudat Israel*				13,799	2.0	3	39,836	4.7	6
Poalei Agudat Israel*				11,194	1.6	2			
Herut	49,782	11.5	14	45,651	6.6	8	107,190	12.6	15
Israel Communist Party	15,148	3.5	4	27,334	4.0	5	38,492	4.5	6
Progressives	17,786	4.1	5	22,171	3.2	4	37,661	4.4	5
Israel Arab Democrats	7,387	1.7	2	16,370	2.4	3	15,475	1.8	2
Sephardic Oriental Communities	15,287	3.5	4	12,002	1.8	2	6,994	0.8	0
Progress and Work (Arab)	—	—	—	8,067	1.2	1	12,511	1.5	2
Yemenites	4,399	1.0	1	7,965	1.2	1	2,448	0.3	—
Agriculture and Development (Arab)	—	—	—	7,851	1.1	1	9,791	1.1	1
Fighters (Lohamim)	5,363	1.2	1	—	—	—	—	—	—
WIZO	5,173	1.2	1	—	—	—	—	—	—
Other various Jewish tickets	13,198	3.4	—	4,413	0.6	—	16,133	1.9	—
Other various Arab tickets	6,026	1.3	—	—	—	—	4,484	0.5	—
Eligible voters	506,567			924,885			1,057,795		
Total voting	440,095			695,007			876,085		
Canceled votes	5,411			7,515			22,866		
Voting participation	86.9%			75.4%			82.8%		

* These four parties presented one list, the United Religious Bloc, at 1949 election; they ran on separate lists in the elections for the Second Knesset; and in the Third Knesset elections the Mizrahi and Agudah parties each ran on a combined list with its labor affiliate.

— Reading No. 24 —

COMPOSITION OF GOVERNMENTS OR CABINETS (BY PARTIES)[24]

Provisional Government
May 15, 1948-March 10, 1949

Mapai	4
General Zionists	2
Mapam	2
Mizrahi	1
Agudat Israel	1
Hapoel Hamizrahi	1
Progressives	1
Sephardim	1
	—
	13

First Government
March 10, 1949-November 1, 1950

Mapai	7
United Religious Front	3
Progressives	1
Sephardim	1
	—
	12

Second Government
November 1, 1950-October 8, 1951

Mapai	7
United Religious Front	3
Progressives	1
Sephardim	1
Non-Members of Knesset	1
	—
	13

Third Government
October 8, 1951-December 24, 1952

Mapai	9
Hapoel Hamizrahi	2
Agudat Israel	1
Mizrahi	1
	—
	13

[24] Author's listing.

Fourth Government
December 24, 1952-January 26, 1954

Mapai	9
General Zionists	4
Hapoel Hamizrahi	2
Progressives	1
	—
	16

Fifth Government
January 26, 1954-June 29, 1955

Mapai	9
General Zionists	4
Hapoel Hamizrahi	2
Progressives	1
	—
	16

Sixth Government
June 29-November 3, 1955

Mapai	8
Hapoel Hamizrahi	2
Progressives	1
Non-Members of Knesset	1
	—
	12

Seventh Government
November 3, 1955-December 31, 1957

Mapai	8*
Hapoel Hamizrahi–Mizrahi	2
Progressives	1
Mapam	2
Ahdut Avodah–Poale Zion	1
Non-Members of Knesset	2
	—
	16

Eighth Government
January 7, 1958—

Same as Seventh Government

* On June 18, 1956, Moshe Sharett left the Government, but another Mapai member was added.

— Reading No. 25 —

GROWTH OF COLLECTIVE AND COOPERATIVE AGRICULTURAL SETTLEMENTS, 1946-1956 [25]

TYPE OF SETTLEMENT	1946		1956	
	NUMBER	POPULATION	NUMBER	POPULATION
Kibbuts and *Kvutzah*	140 (in 1945)	Over 40,000	223	81,300
Workers Smallholders' Settlement (*Moshav Oydim*)	62	17,099	101 ⎫	
Immigrant Smallholders' Settlement (*Moshav Olim*)	—	—	182 ⎭	93,000
Collective Smallholders' Settlement (*Moshav Shitufi*)	9	878	20	3,082

[25] This table is based on State of Israel, Ministry of Labour, *Cooperative Societies in Israel, 1956* (Jerusalem, 1957) pp. 11, 13, 15, and on the listing of all Jewish settlements and their social structure in 1946, in *Statistical Handbook of Jewish Palestine,* cited, pp. 411-426.

— Reading No. 26 —

BALANCE OF TRADE, 1949-1956 (IN MILLIONS OF DOLLARS)[26]

The following table presents the latest figures (in American dollars) of the Israeli Central Bureau of Statistics, which has recalculated previous data at the single rate of exchange of £I 1.800 = $1.00. The figures given in American dollars by other sources vary because of older calculations at varying rates of exchange.

✔   ✔   ✔

YEAR	IMPORTS	EXPORTS	TRADE DEFICIT (EXCESS OF IMPORTS OVER EXPORTS)	EXPORTS AS PERCENT OF IMPORTS
1949	253.1	29.7	223.4	11.7
1950	298.8	36.9	261.9	12.3
1951	379.8	46.8	333.0	12.3
1952	321.1	44.4	276.7	13.8
1953	281.2	59.7	221.5	21.2
1954	286.5	88.1	198.4	30.8
1955	325.0	90.2	234.8	27.8
1956	364.0	107.2	256.7	29.5

[26] State of Israel, Central Bureau of Statistics, *Statistical Abstract of Israel, 1956-1957*, p. 159.

— Reading No. 27 —

TRIPARTITE (FRANCE, THE UNITED KINGDOM, AND THE UNITED STATES) DECLARATION OF MAY 25, 1950[27]

Tension continued in the Middle East after the partition of Palestine. The Arab states talked openly of a second round in the struggle with Israel, and hostility between Jordan and the other Arab states mounted as a result of the enlargement of Jordan's territory. The following declaration was issued as a warning against attacks upon Jordan as well as against a resumption of war upon Israel.

✓   ✓   ✓

The Governments of the United Kingdom, France and the United States, having had occasion during the recent Foreign Ministers meeting in London to review certain questions affecting the peace and stability of the Arab states and of Israel, and particularly that of the supply of arms and war material to these states, have resolved to make the following statements:

1. The three Governments recognize that the Arab states and Israel all need to maintain a certain level of armed forces for the purposes of assuring their internal security and their legitimate self-defence and to permit them to play their part in the defence of the area as a whole. All applications for arms or war material for these countries will be considered in the light of these principles. In this connection the three Governments wish to recall and reaffirm the terms of the statements made by their representatives on the Security Council

[27] *Department of State Bulletin*, XXII (June 5, 1950), p. 886.

on 4th August, 1949, in which they declared their opposition to the development of an arms race between the Arab States and Israel.

2. The three Governments declare that assurances have been received from all the States in question, to which they permit arms to be supplied from their countries, that the purchasing State does not intend to undertake any act of aggression against any other State. Similar assurances will be requested from any other States in the area to which they permit arms to be supplied in the future.

3. The three Governments take this opportunity of declaring their deep interest in and their desire to promote the establishment and maintenance of peace and stability in the area, and their unalterable opposition to the use of force or threat of force between any of the States in that area. The three Governments, should they find that any of these States was preparing to violate frontiers or armistice lines, would, consistently with their obligations as members of the United Nations, immediately take action, both within and outside the United Nations, to prevent such violation.

— Reading No. 28 —

ISRAEL'S BLUEPRINT FOR PEACE[28]

On December 1, 1952, Ambassador Abba Eban delivered an address before the Ad Hoc *Political Committee of the United Nations General Assembly, outlining in considerable detail the bases of Arab-Israel peace. The*

[28] Abba Eban, *Peace in the Middle East* (New York: Israel Office of Information, n. d.), pp. 3-35. This address is included in *Idem, Voice of Israel* (New York, 1957), pp 93-122. A summary of the address is given in United Nations, Seventh Session of General Assembly, *Official Records* (December 1, 1952), pp. 165-171.

following extracts present the main points of this comprehensive address.

✓   ✓   ✓

. . . Israel has faced many pre-occupations in the past five years of her national independence. . . . Although these concerns have all pressed upon us simultaneously and together, we have never lost sight of our chief objective—the attainment of peace in our region.
Today Israel is prepared to make the attainment of peace in its region a primary theme of its national policy, and to bring all its resources to bear upon that task. . . .
The relations between Israel and the Arab States have six major aspects, all of which should figure on the agenda of direct peace negotiations. . . . (1) Security questions; (2) Territorial questions; (3) Refugee questions; (4) Economic questions; (5) Regional Cooperation: communications, social and health questions, scientific and cultural questions, technical assistance cooperation; (6) Questions of diplomatic and juridical relations. . . .

I. SECURITY QUESTIONS

. . . It is, therefore, my Government's belief that a peace negotiation should contain four elements under the security heading:
First, the peace settlement should include a non-aggression clause. . . . We have heard assertions that the Arab states on their part profess a fear of Israel expansion. Here I would give assurance that these fears are quite unfounded. . . .
Second, such a settlement would enable a reasonable limitation of military budgets and the avoidance of competitive re-armament. . . .
Third, the transition from armistice to a peace settlement would eliminate local outbreaks and violence along the frontiers through armed incursions and infiltrations. . . .
Fourth, the settlement here envisaged would enable the states of the Near East to survey methods of regional cooperation for strengthening peace in the area, within the terms of the United Nations Charter. . . .

II. TERRITORIAL QUESTIONS

. . . The peace negotiation would enable the parties

to exchange proposals on the manner in which the arr
istice frontiers might be mutually adjusted for a peace se
tlement. One of the problems to be considered would
the elimination of demilitarized zones, where division
obscurity of authority has caused great tensions at critic
times. It would also enable adjustments to be made,
suitable exchanges, for reuniting certain villages with th
lands and fields in cases where the armistice frontiers no
separate them. . . .

III. REFUGEE QUESTIONS

. . . I would state again that this tragic suffering is t
legacy of the war against Israel and, therefore, the r
sponsibility of those who initiated that war. This co
sideration in no way affects the profound anxiety a
concern with which the Government and people of Isra
have observed the languishing of these unhappy victims
refugee camps. . . . [Mr. Eban then stated that, desp
the hostility of the Arab States, Israel had released block
accounts held by Arab refugees in Israeli banks; and th
it had recently undertaken responsibility for the integ
tion into Israel of 19,000 Arab refugees. On the questi
of compensation, he said that Israel had cooperated w
the Conciliation Commission] in making available t
records on which a study of the compensation questi
may be pursued. . . . One of the chief factors whi
affect Israel's capacity of payment is the boycott a
blockade imposed by Arab states. Thus, the negotiation
this peace settlement, by removing those abnormal co
ditions, would have a direct bearing on the degree a
rate of progress in payment of compensation. . . .

IV. ECONOMIC QUESTIONS

[Mr. Eban suggested the following areas of possi
economic cooperation: replacement of boycott and bloc
ade by normal economic relations; the development
raw materials and markets for industrial products; jo
irrigation schemes; and reclamation of desert areas.]

V. REGIONAL COOPERATION

[Mr. Eban went on to describe the possible benefits
regional cooperation in communications, public hea
and sanitation, scientific and cultural intercourse, a
technical assistance.]

In the context of a peace settlement there would be no justification for portraying the southern part of Israel as though it were some kind of a "wedge" between various parts of the Arab World. . . . Indeed, within the context of the settlement which I am here presenting, Israel would regard itself as a bridge and not as a wedge.

VI. DIPLOMATIC AND JURIDICAL RELATIONS

This final item in the proposed pattern of new relations is the framework for all the others. The establishment of normal relations, in all the fields which I have outlined, should be given formal effect in diplomatic instruments. There should be a declaration abandoning the unilateral theory of a state of war. . . . Treaties of peace should replace the armistice agreements. The boycott and blockade should be succeeded by trade treaties and transit agreements. Treaties of commerce, navigation and friendship should replace the ostracism and silence which mark our relationship today. Air agreements, visa agreements and the conventions which normally exist between sovereign states at peace with each other should be negotiated. . . .

Such is the general outline of a peace negotiation: security guarantees and cooperation; agreed territorial adjustments; joint consideration of the refugee question with immediate preparatory work on compensation; economic cooperation, including joint water projects and development schemes; regional cooperation, including the opening of access to ports and renewal of direct intercommunication between all parts of the Arab world; formulation of peace treaties and trade pacts. . . .

A SHORT BIBLIOGRAPHY

Baratz, J., *A Village by the Jordan* (London, 1954).

Sharer, S., *The Magic Carpet* (New York, 1952).

Begin, M., *The Revolt: Story of the Irgun* (New York, 1951).

Bein, A., *Theodor Herzl* (Philadelphia, 1941).

Ben Gurion, D., *Rebirth and Destiny of Israel* (New York, 1954).

Bernadotte, F., *To Jerusalem* (London, 1951).

Bernstein, M., *The Politics of Israel* (Princeton, 1957).

Bonné, A., *State and Economics in the Middle East*, 2nd ed. (London, 1955).

Cohen, I., *A Short History of Zionism* (London, 1951)

Davis, M., *Israel: Its Role in Civilization* (New York 1956).

Dunner, J., *The Republic of Israel* (New York, 1950).

Eban, A., *Voice of Israel* (New York, 1957).

Eisenstadt, S., *The Absorption of Immigrants* (London 1954).

Elath, E., *Israel and Her Neighbors* (New York, 1957)

Esco Foundation for Palestine, *Palestine: A Study o, Jewish, Arab and British Policies*, 2 vols. (New Haven 1947).

Eytan, W., *The First Ten Years* (New York, 1958).

Gamzu, H., *Painting and Sculpture in Israel* (Tel Aviv 1951).

Garcia-Granados, J., *The Birth of Israel* (New York 1948).

Gradenwitz, P., *Music and Musicians in Israel* (Jerusalem 1952).

Gruber, R., *Israel To-day* (New York, 1958).

Halkin, S., *Modern Hebrew Literature* (New York 1950).

Hanna, P., *British Policy in Palestine* (Washington 1942).

Horowitz, D., *State in the Making* (New York, 1953).

Huebner, T., and Voss, C., *This Is Israel* (New York 1956).

Hurewitz, J. C., *Diplomacy in the Near and Middle East* II (Princeton, 1956).

————, *The Struggle for Palestine* (New York, 1950)

Israel and the United Nations (New York, 1956).

Kallen, H. M., *Utopians at Bay* (New York, 1958).

Kimche, J., *Seven Fallen Pillars* (New York, 1953).

Kraines, O., *Israel: The Emergence of a New Natio* (Washington, 1954).

Kurland, S., *Cooperative Palestine: The Story of th Histadrut* (New York, 1947).

aqueur, W., *Communism and Nationalism in the Middle East* (New York, 1956).

ehrman, H., *Israel: The Beginning and Tomorrow* (New York, 1951).

evensohn, L., *Vision and Fulfillment* (New York, 1950).

evin, H., *I Saw the Battle of Jerusalem* (New York, 1950).

itvinoff, B., *Ben-Gurion of Israel* (New York, 1954).

cDonald, J. G., *My Mission in Israel* (New York, 1951).

onograph on Community Settlements and Report of the Survey Mission on Community Organization and Development in Israel (United Nations, 1954).

atai, R., *Israel Between East and West* (Philadelphia, 1953).

eretz, D., *Israel and the Palestine Arabs* (Washington, 1958).

abinowicz, O. K., *Fifty Years of Zionism* (London, 1952).

——, *Herzl, Architect of the Balfour Declaration* (New York, 1958).

ackman, E., *Israel's Emerging Constitution* (New York, 1955).

evusky, A., *Jews in Palestine* (New York, 1945).

.I.I.A., *Great Britain and Palestine* (London, 1946).

osenne, S., *Israel's Armistice Agreements with the Arab States* (Tel Aviv, 1951).

acher, H., *Israel: The Establishment of a State* (New York, 1952).

chechtman, J., *The Arab Refugee Problem* (New York, 1952).

hwadran, B., *The Middle East, Oil and the Great Powers* (New York, 1955).

eiser, E. A., *The United States and the Near East* (Cambridge, Mass., 1950).

piegel, S., *Hebrew Reborn* (New York, 1930).

yrkin, M., *Way of Valor* (New York, 1955).

allenrod, R., *The Literature of Modern Israel* (New York, 1956)

eizmann, C., *Trial and Error* (London, 1949).

illiams, L., *The State of Israel* (London, 1957)

INDEX

VAN NOSTRAND ANVIL BOOKS already published